Tennessee Governors at Home

Jennifer - it is fun to
have you at the Assembly
this summer.

Best wishes

Riddley

July 2000

Also by Ridley Wills II

Touring Tennessee: A Postcard Panorama (1996)

Old Enough to Die (1996)

A Brief History of the YMCA
of Nashville and Middle Tennessee (1996)

A Walking Tour of Mt. Olivet Cemetery (1993)

The History of Belle Meade: Mansion, Plantation, and Stud (1991)

Belle Meade Bloodlines, 1816–1904 (1990)

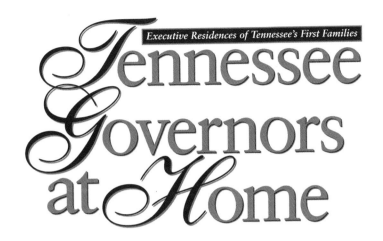

Executive Residences of Tennessee's First Families

Tennessee Governors at Home

Ridley Wills II

HILLSBORO PRESS

FRANKLIN, TENNESSEE

TENNESSEE HERITAGE LIBRARY
Bicentennial Collection

Printed in the United States of America

03 02 01 00 99   1 2 3 4 5

Library of Congress Catalog Card Number: 99-66045

ISBN: 1-57736-073-7

Cover design by Gary Bozeman

Published by
HILLSBORO PRESS
An imprint of
PROVIDENCE HOUSE PUBLISHERS
238 Seaboard Lane • Franklin, Tennessee 37067
800-321-5692
www.providencehouse.com

TO

WILLIAM RIDLEY WILLS

the grandfather I wish I had known
and for whom I was named

CONTENTS

FOREWORD

TENNESSEE'S EXECUTIVE RESIDENCE IS CELEBRATING A VERY important anniversary this year, 1999. It has been seventy years since the home was built by William Ridley Wills. It has also been fifty years since the house was purchased by the state to be a home for Tennessee's governors and their families. I am thankful that, after his initial reluctance, Governor Gordon Browning had the foresight to encourage the General Assembly to purchase this magnificent residence.

Tennessee executive residence. TPS

Ever since Don and I moved in, I have been fascinated by the stories that other governors' families have shared with me about their years here. Many of our guests also have told about events they attended in the past or about changes they have seen made in the residence or on the grounds. I especially enjoyed the story of Ida Browning, the governor's wife who didn't like the newfangled stove and wanted her wood cookstove brought back.

I thought it was important that these individual stories of family life be recorded and preserved while

ix

First Lady Martha Sundquist in the executive residence garden. TPS

so many of the families were still living in the Nashville area. I approached Ridley Wills II about writing the book since it was his grandfather who built the house.

Being a historian and writer he would be able to appreciate the historical significance of having these stories recorded. He also knows more about the house than anyone else. I was thrilled when he agreed to undertake the project of interviewing the former first families and telling their tales.

I hope you will enjoy getting to know these families as real people leading normal lives under not-so-normal circumstances. You will read about young children playing in the halls and attics as well as formal dinners with U.S. presidents. You will celebrate the holidays with different family customs. And you will learn of the changes made to the interior decor as well as to the beautiful ten acres that surround the home, land which I have come to love.

My deepest thanks to Ridley for his commitment to this book which has been a dream of mine for four years. It would not have come to fruition without him.

Martha Sundquist
Fall 1999

PREFACE AND ACKNOWLEDGMENTS

Seated (left to right): Ellen Wills, Phoebe Clark, Ridley Wills II, and Matt Wills. Standing: Eleanor Clark. Far Hills, 1940. RWII

MARTHA SUNDQUIST NATURALLY FLATTERED ME BY HER expression of confidence in my ability to write this book. I immediately accepted the task because, from the time I was born in 1934 until January 1949 when my grandmother sold her home to the State of Tennessee for its executive residence, I went to "Far Hills" nearly every Sunday after church. The family members who gathered to have dinner with my grandmother, Jessie Ely Wills, were my parents, Ellen and Jesse Wills; my brother and sister, Matt and Ellen Wills; my aunt, Mamie Craig Crook and her husband, Senter C. Crook; and my first cousins—Eleanor Clark, Phoebe Clark, and George Wills Crook.

The generous person who made all this possible—my grandfather, William Ridley Wills—had a nervous breakdown in 1938 and was never, thereafter, able to enjoy his wonderful home with his children and grandchildren. I now believe that he was manic-depressive and suspect that it was in one of his periods of euphoria that he built "Far Hills."

Jessie Ely (Mrs. W. Ridley) Wills. RWII

Certainly, he did not need to build such a large home as his only daughter, Mamie Craig, had been married since 1925 to her first husband, C. P. "Ted" Clark. My grandparents' only son, Jesse E. Wills, married the former Ellen Buckner on June 17, 1930. So, when my grandparents moved into their new home in the summer of 1931, their grown

children lived elsewhere. I have always been proud that, in 1931, my grandfather also built Haywood County Memorial Hospital in his hometown of Brownsville, Tennessee, in memory of his parents, Dr. and Mrs. William Thaddeus Wills.

One of the greatest satisfactions I receive from writing any book involves the people I meet and get to know as I go about my research. It would have been impossible to capture the flavor of the lives of Tennessee's first families had I not been able to talk with our present governor, Don Sundquist; three former governors, Lamar Alexander, Winfield Dunn, and Ned McWherter; as well as numerous first family members and descendants. Heading that list is Martha Sundquist, who was always ready to help and whose idea this book was. Her assistant, Anne Locke, always returned my telephone calls promptly and invariably garnered whatever photographs or information I needed. Much appreciation to Jed DeKalb, chief state photographer, for his assistance in securing official photos of the Sundquists and of former administrations.

One of the first people I interviewed for this book was my friend, Hortense Cooper. My wife, Irene, and I visited with her one summer day at the Coopers' handsome home in Shelbyville. Hortense did an excellent job proofreading the section of the book about her late husband, Governor Prentice Cooper. Later, Tom Hudson, Walter M. Robinson Jr., and Margaret Sloan, all of Nashville, added interesting stories about Governor Cooper.

How much fun it was for me to discover that my friend, Robin Merritt, is a great-granddaughter of Malcolm Patterson, the first Tennessee governor to live in an official executive residence. She helped on several occasions. The four interior photographs of the John P. Williams home, which became our first executive residence in 1907, have never been published before. Amelia Edwards, of Nashville, found the negatives which Ruth Warner, of Nashville, a great-granddaughter of Mr. and Mrs. Williams, graciously allowed me to use. Betty Caldwell, of Nashville, provided me several good stories about her grandfather, Governor Tom C. Rye. Andrew Jackson York, of Pall Mall, Tennessee, and Dr.

TENNESSEE GOVERNORS AT HOME

Michael Birdwell, of Tennessee Technological University, were helpful in providing the photograph of Sgt. Alvin York when he and his wife, Gracie, visited The Hermitage while on their honeymoon in Nashville.

How pleased and surprised I was to locate and talk with so many of the grandchildren of Governor Alfred Taylor. Benjamin Harrison Taylor Jr. of Gray, Tennessee, and Landon Taylor, of Nashville, were among numerous Taylor family members who readily answered my questions. When I could not find a photograph of the governor's mansion on West End Avenue, my friend, Ann Reynolds, of the Metropolitan Historical Commission, lent me one. To find out more about Governors Buford Ellington, Henry Horton, and Jim McCord, I visited the Marshall County Memorial Library in Lewisburg, Tennessee. The director, Mrs. Charlene Nicholas, readily agreed to make a copy of the library's photograph of Mrs. Henry Horton for my book. I am grateful for that courtesy. My cousin, Donald U. Bathrick Jr., and his wife, Grace, helped both with photographs and stories about his grandparents, Governor and Mrs. Hill McAlister.

Having Congressman Bob Clement and his brother, Judge Frank G. Clement Jr., take the time to read the chapter entitled "The Leapfrog Years" was especially comforting. Without their help I would have missed several good stories about their father. Dan Pomeroy, director of collections at the Tennessee State Museum, helped me with pictures for this chapter. Several members of the Andrew Benedict Jr. family, who lived across the street from the executive residence, also helped me with stories about their relationships with several of Tennessee's first families. Ann Ellington Wagner, Governor Ellington's daughter, was particularly nice to share information about her family when they lived on Curtiswood Lane. Her 1961 photograph of herself and Elvis Presley was an unexpected dividend. Mary Smith, Robert N. Moore Jr., and Eddie Jones, all of Nashville, also added colorful stories regarding "The Leapfrog Years."

A bonus of writing this book was getting to know Governor and Mrs. Winfield Dunn better. How gracious and accommodating they both were. One day I enjoyed having lunch in the Capitol Grille at the Hermitage Suite Hotel with Betty Blanton and her daughter, Debbie Blanton Flack. They were, then and later, just as helpful as they could be. Another luncheon, which I both appreciated and enjoyed, was with Honey Alexander, Carole Martin Willis, and Debbie Koch. They were great about making sure that I got the story of the Alexander years correct. Ida Finch and Jean Searcy were also valuable resources in this regard.

My special thanks to Robin Hood, the founding director of Tennessee Photographic Services, for his candid photographs of the Alexander family.

In writing the section on Governor McWherter, I received much input both from him and from his son, Mike. Governor McWherter is a charming man who is not nearly as intimidating as his stature would suggest. Two friends of mine, Walter G. Knestrick and Irby Simpkins, told me stories that also helped make chapter 9 more interesting. Lois Riggins-Ezzell, of the Tennessee State Museum, also assisted me with this chapter.

Others, not already mentioned, who helped in making this book possible are as follows:

From Tennessee Photographic Services—Tom Dekle, state photographer II and Earl Warren Jr., former director; from the Tennessee State Museum—Evadine O. McMahan, director of administration and James A. Hoobler, senior curator of art and architecture; from the Tennessee State Museum Foundation, Inc.—Neil Rasmussen III, director and chief financial officer; and from the Tennessee State Library and Archives—Charles A. Sherrill, director of public service; Wayne Moore, manuscript archivist; Susan Gordon, Genella Olker, and Julia Rather, archivists.

Abbreviations were used for the following individuals and organizations who provided materials and illustrations for this book:

AP
Associated Press

DUB
From the collection of Mr./Mrs. Donald U. Bathrick Jr.

JCG/MFC
From the collection of Judy Cisco Gentry/ Mary Frances Cisco

MHC
Metro Historical Commission

NRM
From the collection of Ned Ray McWherter

RJW
From the collection of Mrs. Robert J. Warner

RWII
From the collection of Ridley Wills II

THS
Tennessee Historical Society

TPS
Tennessee Photographic Services

TSLA
Tennessee State Library and Archives

TSM
Tennessee State Museum

WD
From the collection of Winfield Dunn

Finally, I want to thank Andrew B. Miller and the staff at Providence House Publishers for their valuable work—especially Stephen B. James, Holly Jones, Debbie Sims, Lacie Dotson, Marilyn Friedlander, and Mary Bray Wheeler.

There were many others with whom I spoke about *Tennessee Governors at Home.* I appreciate their help and their comments.

PART ONE
1796–1948

CHAPTER ONE
THE YEARS WITHOUT

WHEN TENNESSEE WAS ADMITTED TO THE FEDERAL UNION in 1796 as its sixteenth state, John Sevier, a noted Indian fighter and former governor of the ill-fated State of Franklin, was elected governor. Knoxville was selected as the first state capital. This was an easy choice since Knoxville had been capital of the Territory South of the River Ohio and since East Tennessee then contained more than four times as many inhabitants as did the central part of the state, then called West Tennessee. Present-day West Tennessee was still Indian territory. With his election as Tennessee's first governor, John Sevier moved his family from their log home on the Nolichucky River to the Knoxville area. Instead of building a home in town where there would be protection from Indians, Sevier chose a site across the Holston River five miles in the direction of the Cherokee villages on the Little Tennessee River. There he built a simple log home and there he held office. Later, while still serving as governor, Sevier began building a two-story Federal house in Knoxville which

Home of Tennessee's first governor, John Sevier, near Knoxville, Tennessee. RWII

was still unfinished when he died. There is a tradition that he also lived for some time in a house on Knoxville's Central Avenue.[1] In all the years that the state capital remained at Knoxville, Tennesseans never felt it necessary to construct a building to house the state government. During those years, the governor's office was always in the governor's house. Similarly, it would not be until 1907, 111 years after Sevier was first elected governor, that the General Assembly of the State of Tennessee would establish an executive residence for its chief executive.

Until Nashville was designated as the permanent capital of Tennessee in 1843, little thought had been given toward constructing a State Capitol building, much less acquiring a governor's residence. The problem was that the capital of the state kept moving—from Knoxville to Kingston for one day in 1807, then back to Knoxville before moving to Nashville in 1812.[2] The next move was back to Knoxville in 1817. That city's status as capital of Tennessee came to an end when Murfreesboro was designated as the seat of state government. The

From an early postcard. The Tennessee State Capitol, Nashville, Tennessee. RWII

General Assembly met in Murfreesboro from 1819 to 1826, when the capital moved to Nashville. On October 7, 1843, after a long and bitter fight, Nashville was chosen as the permanent capital of Tennessee.[3]

In Knoxville, the legislature first met in a house.[4] The General Assembly also met in a tavern for a period of time. In Kingston, the General Assembly met for one day in a session that probably lasted less than two hours. The meeting was held in a two-story frame house. In Murfreesboro, the General Assembly met first in the courthouse, until it burned, and

then in the Presbyterian Church.[5]

The first legislator to propose a residence for the governor of Tennessee was Dr. Samuel Bowen Moore of Hickman County. In 1850, he proposed that the legislature's Committee on Public Buildings "inquire into and report on the propriety of purchasing a residence to be kept and held for the use of the governors of Tennessee."[6] The legislature took no action on the matter.

For the next fifty-seven years, various bills, resolutions, and amendments were introduced into the General Assembly reflecting legislative concern over the

TENNESSEE GOVERNORS AT HOME

subject of housing and housing expenses for the governor. Unless they were Nashvillians, the governors normally lived either in Nashville hotels or in rooming houses, usually with inadequate housing allowances. Andrew Johnson was an exception in that he had a home on the corner of Vine and Demonbreun Streets in Nashville during his first term as governor and another home at 58 Cedar Street when he was occupation governor. Governor Isham Harris, an ardent secessionist who served as governor 1857–1862, normally lived at the City Hotel. Nevertheless, in February 1862, only days before Nashville fell to Union forces, a correspondent for *Harper's Weekly* found "Governor Harris in a little shanty opposite the State Capitol which was used by the architects during its construction." The scribe went on to write, "He is too mean to take lodgings at a hotel."[7]

Perhaps the most interesting of the various nineteenth-century housing proposals set forth was one to remodel the old lunatic asylum for an executive residence. In 1860, Senator R. W. Bumpas introduced Senate Bill No. 217 to appropriate the building which

the state owned, and which had, since 1851, been operated as the city hospital. Bumpas's idea was to remodel the building for the gubernatorial residence. He felt his proposal would not cost the state a dime since he also proposed that, except for two acres surrounding the building, part of which would be reserved for a garden, the grounds would be sub-divided into lots and then sold at auction with the proceeds used to repair and remodel the asylum. In February 1860, word of the proposal leaked out. The medical faculty of the University of Nashville heard about it and filed a vehement protest with the legislature. The eight medical school professors who signed the protest had clout. Three of them were future presidents of the

ABOVE: Andrew Johnson, Tennessee governor and seventeenth president of the United States. THS/TSM

TOP: The Tennessee State Legislature once met in this rented Knoxville building. RWII

Governor Isham Harris's birthplace near Tullahoma, Tennessee. RWII

American Medical Association. The high regard in which they were held in the medical community and in Nashville, along with divided sentiment in the General Assembly, doomed the bill which had earlier been thought to have a good chance of passage. The senate voted for the bill, with amendments, 14 to 7, but the house rejected the bill by a vote of 32 to 27. So, by a slim majority, the General Assembly rejected the idea of establishing the "'old Lunatic Asylum' as a St. Helena for the banishment of future governors of the State."[8]

On Christmas Eve 1863, when Andrew Johnson was military governor, he held an open house at his home on Cedar Street for the senior military officers in the city. Standing near the piano in the reception room of his home, he received Federal Generals U.S. Grant, William T. Sherman, Phillip Sheridan, Robert S. Granger, Grenville M. Dodge and others. Several of the officers, some of whom entered the house wearing blouses under army overcoats, apologized for their frayed uniforms as the governor "quizzically eyed his visitors' clothes."[9]

The Civil War interrupted any serious thought of acquiring an executive residence for Tennessee. However, after the war ended, Governor William G. "Parson" Brownlow brought up the subject again. He made a recommendation in October 1865 that The Hermitage, the home of Andrew Jackson, and one hundred acres surrounding it, including Andrew Jackson's tomb, be used as an asylum for invalid soldiers under either state or federal control. The remaining four hundred acres, Brownlow said, should be sold, with the first $70,000 in proceeds used to pay off the state debt on the property. The balance of the funds, he argued, should be used to purchase a mansion for the governor of the state. He identified the George Washington Campbell House on Cedar Street, directly across from the State Capitol, as property which the state should immediately acquire for this purpose. Brownlow made it clear that he would gain no benefit from the purchase but that it should accrue to the benefit of his successors in office. In support of the governor, Senator John Trimble of Davidson County introduced a bill to purchase the home of the late George W. Campbell on Cedar Street and to pay for it with the proceeds of the sale of The Hermitage.[10] After extensive debate, the bill was defeated 13 to 7. While governor, "Parson" Brownlow boarded, part of the time, at 216 Broad Street. When he first took office, he had said that he had to "look out for a cheap boarding house."

Of the other Tennessee governors who served between the Civil War and 1907, most boarded at Nashville hotels. After its completion in 1869, the Maxwell House became the most popular residence for Tennessee governors. So many governors lived there that room number 10 on the mezzanine floor became known as "the Governor's Room."

For several decades, the Maxwell House Hotel was a favorite place of lodging for such Tennessee chief executives as John C. Brown, James D. Porter, Albert Marks, Alvin Hawkins, and Robert Love Taylor. Often it was

The George Washington Campbell House, foreground, on elegant Cedar Street circa 1880, Nashville, Tennessee. RWII

said that a full Tennessee House committee could gather in the fourteen-by-twenty-four-foot room which had a fifteen-foot-high ceiling, a six-foot-wide fireplace, and six broad windows, each ten feet high. The furniture in the room included heavy Victorian beds, marble-top dresser and tables, plush maroon chairs, and matching drapes and rugs.[11] Governor Taylor lived at the Maxwell House during his second term. In his first term (1887–1891), he boarded at the Duncan Hotel. Benton McMillin, James B. Frazier, and John Cox boarded at the Tulane Hotel, while Peter Turney boarded at the Nicholson House, a predecessor hotel to the Tulane. Brownlow's successor, DeWitt C. Senter, boarded at 86 North Summer Street. John Price Buchanan (1891–1893) boarded at 519 Cedar Street while William Bate (1883–1887), a Nashville lawyer, had his own home at 715 Russell Street.

ABOVE: Presidential suite in the Maxwell House Hotel, Nashville, Tennessee. RWII

OPPOSITE: Maxwell House Hotel on the corner of Fourth and Church Streets, Nashville, Tennessee. RWII

In an address to the legislature on January 12, 1891, Robert Love Taylor (who served as governor 1887–1891 and 1897–1899) said:

Now that the time of my retirement is at hand, I can with more propriety urge the purchase or erection by the State of a Mansion House for its governor. The honor in being called to such a high station is ample compensation, but that the State should surround its Executive with facilities for maintaining the dignity of his place and the reputable honor of the commonwealth. It should be furnished and maintained befitting a place where the dignity and honor of the state is lodged.[12]

CHAPTER TWO
THE FIRST OFFICIAL RESIDENCE

O N MARCH 11, 1907, AN EXECUTIVE RESIDENCE WAS FINALLY authorized by the General Assembly of Tennessee. A three-man committee was authorized to secure "a suitable and appropriate executive residence, located conveniently to the Capitol of the State, and within the corporate limits of the City of Nashville."[1] That summer, the former John P. Williams home at 314 Seventh Avenue North (formerly North Vine Street) was purchased for $31,000 from its owner, John M. Gray Jr.[2] Gray, who had owned the home since 1899, was a vice president of Gray & Dudley Hardware and was married to the former Reba Wilson. The Grays were Nashville social leaders. He was also a sportsman, having been involved in bringing the sports of automobile racing and golf to Nashville.[3] Mr. Gray was a charter member of the Nashville Golf and Country Club and served as its first president from 1901 through 1903.[4] The Grays would later build a Georgian colonial-style mansion on Harding Pike next door to Wilmor Manor, the home of Mrs. Gray's parents, Mr. and Mrs. B. F. Wilson.

The east side of Seventh Avenue North with the Governor's Mansion at the far right. From a 1910 era postcard. RWII

Governor's Mansion, 7th Ave., Nashville, Tenn.

11

Since the coming of electric streetcars in 1889, more and more of Nashville's affluent citizens were moving from the old established residential neighborhoods near the State Capitol to newer homes farther from town but still accessible by streetcar on the Fatherland Street, Hillsboro, and West End lines. The shifting residential pattern meant that the state's choice of the Gray house was questionable.

In 1896, G. Malbourne Fogg, who lived at 311 North High Street (Sixth Avenue North), moved to Melrose, a beautiful home on the Franklin Pike. His home on North High became a boardinghouse. The decline of the Sixth and Seventh Avenue North neighborhood was influenced by the division of Polk Place, the former home of Mrs. James K. Polk, into fourteen lots which were then sold at public auction on June 26, 1897.[5] After Judge E. E. East's death in 1902, his beautiful home on North High Street also became a boardinghouse. One after another, other pieces of residential property on Sixth, Seventh, and Eighth Avenues North changed hands, including the elegant house owned by John M. Gray Jr.[6]

Despite this shift in housing patterns, on July 19, 1907, Governor Malcolm R. Patterson moved into the handsome two-story Gray house. The white stone home was large, with drawing and reception rooms on the first floor, along with a library, dining room, and kitchen. The drawing room fireplace had a white and gold mantel framed in onyx, while the room's ceiling was covered with drawings of cupids and roses. These drawings were so special to Mrs. Gray that, when she and her husband sold the house to the state, the contract stipulated that she could remove the ceiling paintings and take them with her. It was said that

ABOVE: The original executive residence on Seventh Avenue North. From an etching by Warren L. Kirbo, Mount Juliet, Tennessee.

TOP: Polk Place, late nineteenth century, Nashville, Tennessee. JCG/MFC

experts from New York tried to remove the canvas from the ceiling but were unable to do so without splitting it. Consequently, the cupids and roses were left for Governor Patterson and his successors to enjoy.[7] The dining room furniture was of hand-carved mahogany. The room featured built-in china cabinets which had stained-glass doors. Fireplaces were in nearly every room, including bathrooms. A daughter of one governor who lived there was delighted to find that her bathroom had a corner fireplace where she could warm her damp feet in front of an open fire. On the second floor there were lots of bedrooms, most with their own baths. On the third floor there was a large ballroom. A stately stairway of hand-carved mahogany, matching the design of the dining room furniture, led from the first to the third floor. Designed by architects Thompson and Gibel, the house had been built by John P. Williams, a Nashville banker and social leader in 1889.[8] He built it especially for the debut of his daughter, Saidee, who was described as "perfectly beautiful." One summer, a young girl in the neighborhood frequently skated up and down Vine

Street in front of the Williams's home. She often seemed to be there when Saidee was entering or leaving. It was later discovered that the little girl was purposely there at such times just so she could look at the lovely Saidee Williams.[9] In 1891, Saidee married Jesse M. Overton.[10]

In 1906, Malcolm Patterson was twice widowed with three small children—Sara, Malcolm Jr., and Elizabeth. He was also a former United States congressman. While campaigning for governor that fall in West Tennessee, he met Miss Mary Russell "Mamie" Gardner, the oldest daughter of Union City's mayor, W. H. Gardner. The next day, Mary presented the gubernatorial candidate with a bouquet of

ABOVE: The front hall of the John P. Williams residence, 314 North Vine Street, Nashville, Tennessee. RJW

TOP: The elaborate drawing room of the John P. Williams residence showing the fireplace with white and gold mantel on the right. RJW

The library of the John P. Williams residence, 314 North Vine Street. From an 1890 photograph. RJW

flowers immediately following his speech in her hometown.[11] She did so with grace and charm, and Malcolm Patterson was quite taken with her. He made it a point to see her again and very quickly a friendship developed that ripened into love. Sometime after their engagement was announced, Patterson, who was by then governor, called Mamie from the new executive residence, the former

TENNESSEE GOVERNORS AT HOME

Governor Malcolm Patterson (center) and his staff at his second inauguration, 1909. Mrs. Patterson and his daughter, Sara, are standing behind Governor Patterson. TSLA

Gray home. He was told that she could not come to the telephone because she and a young man were out on a carriage ride. Governor Patterson was upset and expressed his displeasure when he finally got in touch with Mamie. In response to his complaint, Mamie said, "Malcolm, if you don't trust me now, we better not go any further."[12] Governor Patterson must have reassured his bride-to-be of his trust as, on December 7, 1907, he and Mamie married in her parents' home in Union City. This was only the second time in Tennessee history that a governor married while in office. Trains carrying wedding guests from Memphis and Nashville converged on the West Tennessee town only an hour before the wedding, which was held in the library. Major Eugene C. Lewis came from Nashville in his private railroad car with a group that included Mr. and Mrs.

James C. Bradford; the governor's daughter, Miss Sara Patterson; Miss Libby Morrow; Major Lewis's daughter, Miss Floy Lewis; Colonel Duncan B. Cooper; General Tully Brown; and Mrs. Lucius E. Burch. Following the wedding, which was also attended by prominent business and political figures from across the state, the Pattersons went to Niagara Falls on their honeymoon.[13]

Governor Patterson cherished an opportunity to officially welcome the president of the United States when Theodore Roosevelt arrived by train for a five-hour visit to Nashville and The Hermitage on October 22, 1907. After riding through downtown streets gaily decorated with banners and flags, the presidential carriage and those behind stopped in front of the Ryman Auditorium on Fifth Avenue North. Inside, an enthusiastic crowd heard Governor Patterson make a flowery speech in which he told President Roosevelt that "the men and women who greet you today are Tennesseans to the core, Americans in spirit and purpose, who trace their lineage to the riflemen of King's Mountainage—and no race can claim a nobler heritage." President Roosevelt spoke of his pleasure in being in Nashville and praised the hardy backwoodsmen who settled Tennessee.[14]

Less than one month later, the National Convention of the Woman's Christian Temperance Union (WCTU) was held in Nashville. Governor Patterson welcomed the members during the opening ceremonies at the Ryman Auditorium. The next evening he gave, in their honor, the first public reception ever held in the executive residence. Several hundred delegates attended the gala affair, which took place on Saturday afternoon during a drenching rain. The governor was assisted by his mother, Mrs. Josiah Patterson; Mrs. Benton McMillin; and Mrs. E. C. Adkins. Mrs. Patterson wore a black chiffon and lace over black silk, with diamonds, and held a large bouquet of white roses and maiden hair ferns. She wore black as a sign of respect for her deceased husband, Congressman Josiah Patterson, who died in 1905.[15] Lucille Foster McMillin, the wife of former Governor Benton McMillin, was an extraordinary woman who took a backseat to no one where women's rights were concerned. The daughter of one of the first suffragettes in the South, she was president of the Tennessee Federation of Women's Clubs, a national committeewoman, and regional director of Democratic Women of Southern States.[16] Her dress that afternoon was a cream Renaissance silk over liberty satin with touches of gold on her corsage. She also wore turquoise and diamond jewelry. Mrs. Adkins, who wore a dress of black Canton crepe and thread lace, was state secretary of the Young Woman's Temperance Union. She stood beside Governor Patterson in the front hall and presented the delegates to him as they entered. Patterson, who chatted briefly with each of the delegates, noticed that most of them were without hats. Mrs. Adkins told him that they were deliberately going hatless while in Nashville to call attention to their cause.[17]

Also in the receiving line were Mrs. Lillian M. N. Stevens, the national president of WCTU; Miss Anna Gordon, WCTU vice president; Mrs. Harriet W. Brand, national treasurer; and Mrs. Silena M. Holman, state president. Refreshments were served buffet style in the dining room.

The dining-room table held a centerpiece of rich cluny lace and a central cut-glass bowl holding beautiful white chrysanthemums. Silver dishes and compotes were heaped with confections and wafers. At either end of the table, the governor's daughter, Sara Patterson, and Mrs. Hamilton Parks served tea and chocolate. Sara looked pretty in a white lace and mull gown with touches of green liberty velvet. The drawing rooms on the left side of the hall were elaborately decorated in pure white with chrysanthemums, roses, and carnations against a background of ferns and palms. Before leaving the reception, each of the ladies expressed their appreciation to Governor Patterson for the beautiful entertainment he provided.[18]

Two years later, in 1909, the Tennessee General Assembly passed a bill prohibiting the sale of intoxicating liquors anywhere in the state within four miles of a school. Governor Patterson vetoed the bill, an action which must have perplexed and angered the women who had attended the reception in 1907. Patterson, whom the *Nashville Banner* labeled the "Little Giant of Democracy," insisted he did so

because the people of Tennessee had not been given the opportunity to express themselves on the issue.[19]

Politicians also visited the Pattersons at the executive residence. As a result of a Nashville Boosters' Club visit to Jackson, Mississippi, where the boosters were entertained by Governor E. F. Noel and former Governor James K. Vardeman, these two Mississippians and their wives visited Nashville for Governor's Day at the Tennessee State Fair on September 24, 1908. There, they were welcomed by Governor Patterson as guests of honor. A packed grandstand heard the Tennessee chief executive give a welcoming speech and the Mississippians' responses. That evening, Governor and Mrs. Patterson entertained their prominent guests at a dinner at the executive residence. For the occasion, the Pattersons were joined by Mrs. Patterson's mother, Mrs. W. H. Gardner, of Union City, and by her uncle and aunt, Mr. and Mrs. Thomas Nelson Jones, of Columbia, all of whom spent that night in the mansion. Other dinner guests included former Tennessee Governor Benton McMillin and

his wife; Mrs. John C. Brown, widow of a former Tennessee governor; and Mr. and Mrs. Austin Peay, a future Tennessee governor and his wife. For the occasion, the long drawing room and library were decorated with bouquets of flowers sent to the hosts. The dining room table was covered with "filmy pieces of real lace," and three tall stands of pink roses. Loose pink rosebuds were scattered over the table surface. Each lady present received a long-stemmed pink rose and each gentleman received a pink carnation boutonniere. The place cards were hand painted with pink rose petals and "Tennessee State Fair" in gold shield letters. As the guests ate the six-course dinner, an orchestra provided background music.[20]

During his second term as governor, Malcolm Patterson's wife, Mamie, presented him with a daughter, Mary Gardner Patterson, who was born July 23, 1910, in the executive residence on Seventh Avenue North. Her birth must have been a temporary diversion from his struggles with the prohibition controversy. After his last term ended, Governor Patterson and his family moved back to Memphis and built a

Governor Ben Hooper. From *The Unwanted Boy,* University of Tennessee Press, 1963. TSLA

home where they lived until his death in 1935.

Ben W. Hooper, the second governor to occupy the state's executive residence, was the first actual Republican governor of Tennessee since the Civil War (Governors DeWitt C. Senter and Alvin Hawkins were listed as Whig/Republicans). When elected on a prohibition ticket supported by a coalition of Republicans and Independent Democrats, he and his eight-year-old daughter,

Anna B., came to Nashville and lived in a hotel until he took office. As soon as he was inaugurated in January 1911, the rest of his family followed him to Nashville and settled in the executive residence, which Hooper described as having "been constructed on a rather expensive scale" and being "very ornate, inside and out." He also said that "it had been wisely unloaded on the state for an executive mansion, when all the fine houses in that neighborhood began to be converted into boarding-houses. This happened about the time that the salutary exodus of well-to-do people to rural suburbs set in."[21] The "governor's mansion had no grounds whatever about it," Hooper said, "unless one should be daring enough to denominate about fifteen feet of hopeless, smoke-choked lawn as grounds." Mrs. Hooper agreed with her husband's assessment of the grounds as "smoke-choked." She also was painfully aware of the street dust and garbage odors that were part of city life. The soot from their own and many other coal-burning fireplaces in the city was so intense that the curtains in the executive residence had to be washed each week.[22]

As Governor Hooper fretted about the lack of space surrounding the executive residence, he also faced a similar but more serious problem at the State Capitol. With the growth of state government, there was simply not enough space in the statehouse to accommodate all state offices. The result was that state employees were working in rented or purchased quarters along Cedar Street and Sixth and Seventh Avenues North. In Joint Resolution No. 10, adopted in 1913, the senate and the house appointed a committee to investigate the situation and make recommendations. One charge given the committee was to investigate the advisability of using the executive residence to house some office or department of state government. In case the residence was so used, the committee was charged with determining the cost and location of another suitable building for the residence. Governor Hooper, who obviously was not enamored with the executive residence, was pleased to approve the bill. Nevertheless, nothing came of the proposal with regard to the executive residence during Governor Hooper's term.[23]

Soon after the Hoopers had moved into the executive residence, their two little boys, Ben Jones and Randolph, joined the so-called "Seventh Avenue Gang" and became, according to their father,

skilled warriors in battles wherein limestone macadam was the recognized munition. Ben Jones soon selected as his favorite fighting companion a small colored boy named Grant somebody, who worked in one of the grand old boarding-houses nearby. The colored boy was sturdy and courageous and seemed to consider it a high honor to do battle beside the Governor's boy. Nor could anyone shake Ben Jones' allegiance to his colored friend by teasing him. He insisted that Grant was the best boy on Seventh Avenue, and perhaps he was.[24]

On August 6, 1911, Governor Hooper's wife, the former Anna Bell Jones, gave birth to a son, Lemuel Washington Hooper, their fifth child. The following month, Governor Hooper attended the Tennessee State Fair with other state officials. His daughter, Anna B., whom her father had begun

The Capitol annex was purchased by the State of Tennessee in 1907 to house state offices. RWII

taking with him on trips when she was four, accompanied them.[25] A year after Hooper left office, a baby girl, Newell Sanders Hooper, was born, bringing the number of children in the family to a final total of six, three boys and three girls.[26]

The children of one of Tennessee's governors left such a strong mark on the executive residence on Seventh Avenue that the succeeding governor and his family had to live in a hotel until the mansion could be redecorated and largely refurnished. It seems the children broke a number of

the mansion's beds, used the drawing room as a skating rink, and scrawled crayon pictures on the walls. This sounds as if it might have been the work of the "Seventh Avenue Gang."

During Governor Hooper's two terms of office, Nashville women were campaigning hard for voting rights for females. One day in 1912, the governor's daughter, Anna B. Hooper, then nine years old, marched into Legislative Hall at the State Capitol and announced, "I expect to know as much as my brothers know when we are grown, and I will know as well how to vote as they will." Her father embraced the suffrage cause while little Anna became the darling of school suffrage meetings. At one meeting, she reminded her audience that "ignorant men are allowed to vote, while educated women are denied this privilege. This is not right and every sensible man knows it."[27]

Governor Hooper reluctantly ran for a third term in 1914. He was defeated in the general election by Democrat Thomas C. Rye. When the Hooper family left Nashville the following January, the railroad conductor, who knew perfectly well who Randolph Hooper was, asked the little boy, "Sonny, whose boy are you?" Randolph replied, "I used to be Governor Hooper's boy."[28]

Thomas C. Rye, who defeated Hooper for governor in 1914, was eleven years older than his political rival and not particularly motivated to be governor. At the time of the Democratic convention held in June at the Maxwell House, he came to Nashville out of a sense of duty, but did not bother to attend the session, choosing instead to stay in his hotel room. His son, Paul, who was inter-ested, attended the convention which was held downstairs. Rye gave this account.

Some time after the balloting began, he [Paul] came to my room . . . and declared solemnly, "Dad, they've got you beat." "Thank goodness," I muttered, and prepared to go home. But scarcely were the words out when a convention committee came and told me I had been nominated.[29]

In the general election and at other times, people occasionally asked the Democratic candidate what his middle initial "C" stood for. Rye would laugh and say that it stood for "Tom Cat." Actually, the "C" stood for Clarke. While canvassing the state in 1914, his campaign staff passed out campaign buttons which said "Comin' thru with Rye." They must have been effective as he was elected.[30] Nevertheless, Rye continued to be indifferent to being the chief executive of the state.

Being governor is the most thankless job on earth, and I never did like it very much. One day an old Confederate veteran came into my office and, in a voice loud enough to be heard all over town, extolled his services to the state and demanded that he be given a job. I listened to his story and then got up, walked over to him and pointed to my chair. "I wish I could give you that seat," I said. "It's all I have and I'd be glad to swap."[31]

During Governor Rye's four years as governor, women's suffrage continued to be the key political issue in Tennessee. Rye, who considered himself a father figure in the movement, had some advice for women who, like his wife, Bettie, were in favor of the movement. He told them to begin to work on their antisuffrage sisters. "For, to every anti converted," he said, "that one anti will convert triple the number of men."[32] In an address made in McMinnville, Governor Rye spoke of a minor dispute with his wife at the executive residence over the purchase of two dozen napkins. His wife wanted them made of linen. He wanted nonlinen. The result was that Mrs. Rye got the linen napkins. "Just so in the suffrage question," Governor Rye said. "The women generally know what they want, and go after it."[33]

Gathering for former Governor Rye's birthday, June 1, 1947. Seated: Governor Rye (left) and Governor McCord (right). Standing (left to right): Hallom W. Goodlow, Major Rutledge Smith, Porter Dunlap, and John Nolan. TSLA

Third floor ballroom of the John P. Williams Home, 314 North Vine Street, Nashville, Tennessee, later the first executive residence. From a rare 1890 photo. RJW

Jennings Pharmacy, frequented by Mrs. Rye, located on Church Street at the corner of Seventh Avenue North, Nashville, Tennessee. RWII

While serving as governor, Rye was meticulous about promptly returning any presents given him or his family by constituents. His obsession in this matter so upset his daughter, Nell, that, for the rest of her life, she never got excited about Christmas.[34] One day, someone who thought Governor Rye should be driving a better automobile, brought a new model to the executive residence and dropped off the keys, saying that the automobile was a gift. Naturally, Governor Rye did not accept it.[35]

One of the few presents the Ryes kept was a pair of gray knitted socks with an American flag woven into the front of each. The socks were made by seventy-seven-year-old Mrs. N. P. Koonce, of Fayetteville. She wrote that she "picked the cotton, separated the seed by hand, mixed it with rabbit fur, carded it, spun it, and then knitted them with 'Old Glory' up front where it always ought to be."[36]

Governor Rye, who was considered by his wife to be the "best looking man in the world," habitually went to work wearing a dark suit, white shirt, and black string tie. When he had opportunities to relax at the executive residence on weekends, he enjoyed sitting in a chair by the window, reading and smoking his "smelly old pipe." After stepping down as governor, he recalled that living so close to the State Capitol was both a blessing and a curse. On one hand, the residence was convenient to downtown so Mrs. Rye could easily slip out and walk down to the retail district to shop. It was also fun for family members to sit in the window sills on the back of the house and watch parades on Capitol Boulevard. On the other hand, "the governor's mansion was too conveniently located. People who didn't want to go up the hill to the State Capitol would wait to call on me at night," Governor Rye stated. "I answered the telephone as many as twenty-five times during the night when I was governor." County politicians would come in the executive residence during the day and sit on the elegant white and gold leaf furniture in the long drawing room and gawk at the ceiling paintings of cupids and roses while waiting to see the governor.[37]

After the United States declared war on Germany on April 6, 1917, Governor Rye's son, Paul, then a twenty-one-year-old student at Vanderbilt, decided to join the United States Army as a volunteer. Governor Rye thought that before joining his son needed some drill instruction. Accordingly, he hired someone from the Tennessee National Guard to instruct Paul in basic drills, using the ballroom on the third floor of the executive residence as the drill grounds. For some time, Mrs. Rye and members of her staff had to explain to visitors what the muffled sounds drifting down from the third floor were.[38] During the war, messengers and dignitaries flocked to the mansion all through the night. "I can count on the fingers of one hand all of the nights I slept during the war," said Governor Rye. Finally, in order to get some rest, he hired someone to stay on duty at night to receive messages.[39]

Mrs. Rye was not socially oriented and entertained at the executive residence only as a last resort. In 1946, she recalled that "after I tried to take on four parties on one day and nearly died, I forfeited most events."[40] Bettie Rye was also tight with a dollar and proud of her credit at the nearby Jennings Pharmacy on Church Street. Sometimes, when she had a prescription filled there, she asked the pharmacist to only give her "half a prescription." When the Ryes were preparing to move home to Paris, Tennessee, in 1919, after the governor's second term, the manager of the store confided in Mrs. Rye that she and Governor Rye were the only gubernatorial couple who paid their bills promptly at the first of the month.[41]

After leaving office, Governor Rye refused an offer by President Woodrow Wilson for an appointment to the Court of Customs and Appraisals in New York. Instead, he entered the race for the United States Senate in 1920, which he lost to John K. Shields. He then returned to Paris to practice law. In 1922, he was named chancellor of the Eighth Division of Tennessee and served in that post for twenty years. Governor Rye died at his home in Paris on September 12, 1953, at age ninety.[42]

In 1919, Albert H. Roberts took over the governor's chair, having defeated his Republican opponent, Judge H. B. Lindsey, on a campaign pledge that he would run the government in a conservative and businesslike manner. For all his political prowess, Governor Roberts is best known for performing the wedding ceremony for Sergeant Alvin York, America's greatest World War I hero, and Miss Gracie Williams, known as the "Belle of the Valley of the Three Forks of the Wolf." After Governor Roberts heard that Sergeant York and Gracie were going to be married, he decided that, as governor, he should perform the ceremony. With a politician's instincts, he realized that national publicity would be focused on the wedding and he had an opportunity to share in the spotlight. The arrangement was soon finalized and Governor Roberts was on his way to Pall Mall, Tennessee. Before the wedding on June 7, 1919, Governor Roberts presented York with the uniform of an honorary colonel on the governor's staff. National wire-service reporters estimated the crowd at the wedding to be three thousand. It was held on the

War hero Sgt. Alvin York (in uniform) between his wife, Gracie, and Governor Roberts at The Hermitage. From the collection of the Sgt. Alvin York State Historical Park, Pall Mall, Tennessee.

side of a hill beneath beech trees where Alvin and Gracie had met as sweethearts, near York Spring. York was dressed in his army uniform with the Congressional Medal of Honor and the Croix de Guerre pinned above his left shirt pocket. Miss Williams wore a new dress of light pink silk. Two small front pockets on her dress were decorated with silk handkerchiefs embroidered with silk flags that York had mailed her from France. Before the wedding, Governor Roberts made a speech honoring York's bravery and praising his resistance to opportunities to capitalize on his fame.[43] During the reception, Governor Roberts persuaded York to come to Nashville as his guest on the first leg of Alvin and Gracie's honeymoon. York accepted. The newlyweds; her mother; the two bridesmaids; the Yorks' pastor, Rosier Pile; York's best man, Sergeant Brier; and four other friends of York's came to Nashville on the Tennessee Central from Crossville. This was the first time Gracie and Mother York, who wore a calico sunbonnet for the trip, had ever seen a railroad train.[44] In the capital city, the Yorks were guests of

Governor and Mrs. Roberts in the executive residence. There, Mrs. Roberts explained to Gracie, who was unaccustomed to indoor plumbing, how the guest bathroom worked. While in Nashville, Governor Roberts presented York with a gold and jeweled medal at the executive residence. York was also honored by the Nashville Rotary Club and officially made an honorary colonel on the governor's staff. The party enjoyed a tour of the city, shopping at some of the exclusive shops and women's stores downtown, and visiting The Hermitage, home of another great American soldier. Wednesday night, after a dinner at the Hermitage Hotel, York and his family attended a vaudeville show at the Princess Theater. After the show, the party went to the Fifth Avenue Theater where they saw a silent war movie entitled *Home Town Girl*. They were scheduled to leave the next day for Salt Lake City. However, Pastor Pile convinced York that to go would be "unnecessarily worldly and tempting." York agreed and they canceled the remainder of their honeymoon and, on Thursday, returned to

Crossville by train and from there to Pall Mall by automobile.[45] As she was preparing to leave Nashville, Alvin's mother, who had thoroughly enjoyed herself, never having ventured out of Fentress County before, said that she "intended to come again, when she could go quietly about and really see things—when policemen would not have to make way for her."[46]

Another newly married couple, Congressman Cordell Hull and his bride, the former Rose Frances Whitley, spent several nights in the Seventh Avenue mansion while Roberts was governor. Hull, who was born in Pickett County immediately north of Governor Roberts's home county of Overton, visited the executive residence frequently while Roberts was in office. The Robertses also entertained President Woodrow Wilson's daughter, Margaret.[47] When Dick L. Lansden was appointed chief justice of the Tennessee Supreme Court in 1918, he and his wife temporarily lived with the Robertses in the executive residence until they found a house at 500 North Sixteenth Street in East Nashville.

During his two years in office, Governor Roberts normally did not go out for lunch. Instead, his housekeeper at the residence would walk over to the State Capitol every day with a plate lunch for him. Usually, he ate his lunch "in snatches" as he continued to work at his desk. His wife recalled that Governor Roberts entertained members of the legislature at the executive residence each weekday evening at six, "until every member had been wined and dined."

A week before his gubernatorial term expired, Governor Roberts sent a telegram to incumbent Governor Alfred Taylor advising him that he and his family could move into the residence whenever they wished. About the same time, Mrs. Roberts broke something in the executive residence. In mock despair, she wailed "Oh, I've broken one of Uncle Alfred's andirons."[48]

After leaving public service, Governor Roberts established a very successful law practice in Nashville. Perhaps his greatest case was representing the State of North Carolina in the extradition process against Colonel Luke Lea. Colonel Lea had been resisting extradition to North Carolina following his conviction in 1933 of conspiring to defraud the Central Bank of Asheville, North Carolina, of $300,000.[49]

CHAPTER THREE
THE WEST END YEARS

WHEN GOVERNOR ALFRED TAYLOR, WHO WAS SHORT AND balding, took office in 1921, he was seventy-two years old, about double his age when he unsuccessfully ran for the office against his brother, Bob. A Republican, Alf and his family occupied the executive residence on Seventh Avenue North for only a few months. What disrupted their lives there was that the first executive residence, along with every other house on the east side of the 300 block of the street, was condemned to make way for the War Memorial Building to honor the Tennesseans who fought in the Great War. Consequently, early in his term as governor, Taylor and his family moved to a handsome house the State of Tennessee rented for them at 2118 West End Avenue. Mary E. Tate, the owner, charged the state a rent of $2,500 annually.

In 1921, the Tennessee State Fair was an important event, one at which the governor was expected to make an appearance. Governor and Mrs. Taylor did so. An extra incentive was that the Belle Meade Butter Company had on display during that September event

Likenesses of Governor Alf Taylor and his dog "Old Limber" carved from Belle Meade butter. RWII

29

Governor Alf Taylor (center), 1921, with (left to right) H. A. Morgan, Billy Bond, Andrew Todd, and Judge Sanford. TLSA

The War Memorial Building, Nashville, Tennessee, from an invitation to its dedication, September 21, 1925. RWII

a life-size bust of the governor and a statue of his dog, Old Limber, both made out of pure creamery butter.

While his father was governor, the Taylors' youngest son, Frank "Squirt" Taylor, then about twelve years old, got in a fight with another politician's son. He also got caught by his father making moonshine in the basement of the executive residence with the help of a prison inmate working there. As a result,

Governor and Mrs. Taylor sent Frank to Johnson City to live with their second oldest son, Benjamin Harrison Taylor, who was already married and living there with his wife and baby. Governor Taylor obviously decided that Johnson City would be a better environment than Nashville for their mischevious son, "Squirt," to grow up in. Their oldest son, Nathaniel Taylor, also lived in upper East Tennessee when his father was governor. Both brothers often brought their families to Nashville to visit their parents. Nathaniel's daughter, Florence, who was born in 1914, remem-

bers coming to Nashville and having her grandfather entertain her by playing the fiddle and singing songs in English, French, and German. Florence, in 1998, recalled that her grandmother, Jennie Anderson Taylor, was a lovely lady and a gracious hostess for her husband.[2] Mary and Katherine Taylor, who were among the youngest of the Governor and Mrs. Taylors' nine children, lived at the executive residence while they attended Ward Belmont.[3] One day, Mary was introduced by her brother, Robert "Bob" Taylor, to Carter Williams, his friend and Sigma Alpha Epsilon (SAE) fraternity brother at Vanderbilt. Williams, who had accompanied Bob to the executive residence for a free lunch, later married Mary.[4] Bob Taylor, who also attended law school at Vanderbilt, remembered that his father, whose love for the fiddle was legendary, once invited two fiddle players from Texas to spend the night at the residence. While Governor Taylor worked downstairs during the day, they played their fiddles in an upstairs bedroom. When he felt the urge, Governor Taylor would excuse himself from business and slip upstairs to join them for a few minutes of fiddling pleasure.[5]

While Governor Taylor was in office, a committee of state officials was searching for a successor residence to the one on Seventh Avenue North. One possibility was Burlington, the Italianate home of Mrs. Norman Farrell Jr. on Elliston Place in the heart of Nashville's park district. When Mrs. Farrell died in April 1921, the handsome mansion, built in 1859 by her grandfather, Joseph T. Elliston, and a large plot of land were left to her children and their first cousins. The family consensus was that the house was too expensive to maintain and that it should be sold. Consequently, the

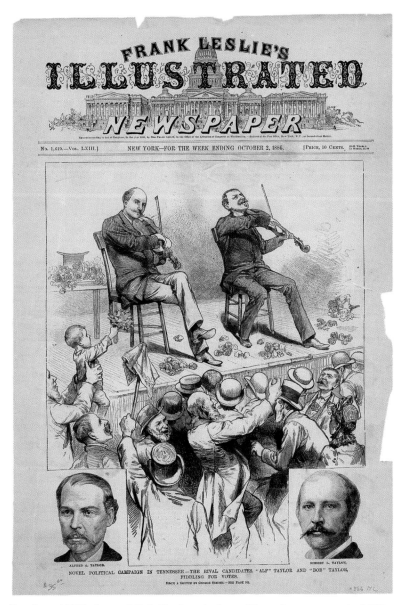

Brothers Alf Taylor and Bob Taylor, rival candidates for governor in 1886, depicted as "fiddling for votes" in a New York newspaper. RWII

Burlington Place. From *Beautiful and Historic Homes in and near Nashville, Tennessee,* by Mrs. James E. Caldwell.

family had a sales brochure produced to market the house. When Mrs. James E. Caldwell, a prominent local preservationist, learned that Burlington would go on the market, she made a public plea for its preservation. Mrs. Caldwell said,

I should like to suggest that effort be made to secure Burlington Place for use as a governor's mansion. It is particularly fitting and of special interest due to the fact that Strickland, the famous architect who designed the Capitol designed Burlington Place also.[6]

Governor and Mrs. Taylor went to see the house. Mrs. Taylor's conclusion was that the fourteen-foot ceilings were too high and that she was not interested.[7]

In spite of his advanced age, Taylor ran for a second term of office in 1922 but was defeated

The second executive residence, previously home of Mary E. Tate, at 2118 West End Avenue, Nashville, Tennessee. MHC

by Austin Peay. "Uncle Alf" retired to live out his life in upper East Tennessee where he enjoyed the company of his wife, Jennie, their large family, and his many friends.

On March 27, 1923, two months after Governor Taylor left office, the state bought the buff-colored Mary E. Tate house that they had been renting for $27,500 "cash."[8] Favorably located across the street from Vanderbilt University, the new executive residence was a squarish, two-story, neoclassical house in one of the city's nicest residential neighborhoods. It had been built in 1910 by Christopher Tompkins Cheek, owner of C. T. Cheek and Company, a wholesale grocery business that Mr. Cheek ran with his sons, Leslie[9] and Will T. Cheek. After C. T. Cheek's

Governor Peay attended many games at Vanderbilt University Stadium. RWII

death in 1915, the house passed into the ownership of Mrs. Tate. It was known for its leaded-glass doors and a handsome dormer-palladium window in the attic. The house was entered through a front hall, to the left of which was a living room. The dining room was to the right. A wide stairway,

accessible from either end, ran at a right angle to the entrance hall and was not immediately visible. A smaller hall at the end of the entrance hall led to the stairways and the kitchen behind. This hall was flooded with light through windows of amber-colored glass at either end. There was also a

bathroom downstairs. Upstairs were bedrooms and one or more baths, while a garage was behind the house on the alley that ran between West End Avenue and Hayes Street.

Austin Peay was the second Tennessee governor, after Governor Taylor, to occupy the executive residence on West End Avenue. When he was inaugurated in January 1923, the state spent $381.25 on the event, including a $20.00 expense for Tony Rose's band, $30.00 to hire horses for the parade, and $7.00 for carnations bought from Geny Brothers Florists.[10]

On September 21, 1925, Governor Peay spoke at the dedication of the War Memorial Building, the structure built by the City of Nashville, Davidson County, and the State of Tennessee on the site of the first executive residence.[11] For years, Governor Peay suffered with high blood pressure and an overworked heart. Consequently, entertaining at the executive residence was not one of his high priorities. Those who were invited there for dinner or a reception found that the governor cracked no jokes and told no funny stories. They were more likely to hear him expound on his interests in tax reform, the completion of the state's long-delayed highway system, the lengthening of the terms of our public schools, the building of more schools, or the importance of preserving Reelfoot Lake and the Great Smoky Mountains as parks.[12] When he

could, Governor Peay visited the Great Smoky Mountains in an effort to promote its use as a national park or, if that failed, a state park. In the summer of 1925, he and his son, Austin Peay Jr., enjoyed a horseback ride in the mountains near Elkmont.[13] Governor Peay also liked to attend athletic events, including Vanderbilt football games. On one or more occasions, he and Charles C. Trabue, of Nashville, watched Vanderbilt football games together. Trabue was both a friend and Peay's attorney. Mrs. Peay enjoyed being a member of the Centennial Club, Nashville's most prestigious women's civic organization. As the first lady of Tennessee, she was named an honorary member in 1923. The following year, Mrs. Peay introduced the club's speaker, Mrs. Izelton Jewel Brown, who gave a speech entitled "The Duty of Women Voters of the State in the Present National Election."[14] Mrs. Peay often accompanied her husband on his trips and campaigns. She became such a part of him that he would often say he could not go unless she went with him.[15]

After completing four years in office, which Governor Peay

Governor and Mrs. Peay on election day, November 1924. From *Austin Peay, Governor of Tennessee*. TSLA

described as "hard, nerve-wearing, and killing years,"[16] he reluctantly ran for and won a third term. On several occasions in the months that followed, Peay confided to friends that he might not live to complete his term. That prophecy came true. On Sunday afternoon, October 2, 1927, as he rested in the executive residence, Governor Peay was stricken with a cerebral hem-

Governor Henry Horton. TSLA

Mrs. Henry Horton. From the Marshall County Memorial Library, Lewisburg, Tennessee.

orrhage. Within three hours he was dead, a victim of overwork and worry and the first governor of Tennessee to die while in office.[17] He was survived by his widow and by two children, Austin Peay Jr. and Amaryllis Peay Armstrong. One of the last persons Governor Peay saw, other than his family, was Truman Hudson Alexander, syndicated columnist for the *Nashville Tennessean*, who served as Peay's unofficial press secretary. Alexander answered a

summons to Peay's bedside in his last hours.[18]

Speaker of the House Henry Horton, a Democrat whom many people called "Uncle Henry," succeeded to the governor's chair upon Austin Peay's death. A native Alabaman, Horton served as governor for the balance of Governor Peay's term and for two terms on his own, October 1927–January 1933. Three weeks after he and Mrs. Horton, the former Anna A. Wilhoite, moved into the executive residence, their

only child, John W. Horton, married. Consequently, there were no children living in the residence during the Horton administration. Happily, in October 1928, John's wife gave birth to a baby daughter, Adeline Wilhoite Horton, named for her grandmother. When the baby was a month old, she made her public debut at the executive residence in the arms of the first lady of Tennessee and surrounded by Christmas seals. Mrs. Horton had purchased the first Christmas seals of the season for her infant granddaughter in hopes that she would grow up "doing something for suffering humanity."[19]

Shortly after his reelection in 1930, Governor Horton found himself in the center of a storm that arose when four banks with large State of Tennessee deposits failed. A legislative committee investigated to determine if there was mismanagement on the part of the state's executive branch. The result was that eight charges of impeachment against Horton were presented in the State House of Representatives. The principal charge was that the governor had conspired with Colonel Luke Lea and Rogers Caldwell to allow them to dominate certain branches of government for their financial gain. In return for this favorable treatment, Horton was allegedly to receive their political support and that of the newspapers they controlled. By a count of 58 to 41, the house voted against impeaching the governor. Nevertheless, the political strife took its toll on Governor Horton, whose health was shattered by what he termed a "pretty hard fight."[20] Because of the economic depression and the fact that he was an ardent prohibitionist of simple habits who retired early and got "up with the sun," Governor and Mrs. Horton seldom entertained. They did enjoy taking automobile rides in the country on Saturday afternoons. When the mood struck him to do so, Governor Horton would often tell his chauffeur, "Let's take out." He picked up the habit of saying this back in his farming days when he would "take out the horse from the plow."[21]

Once, a prominent state senator arrived at the executive residence in the wee hours of the morning without an invitation. It seems that I. D. Beasley, of Carthage, and two of his friends,[22] all members of the state

Mrs. Hill McAlister. DUB

legislature and practical jokesters, decided to play a trick on this important member of the state senate. One cold winter night, sometime after midnight, Beasley, who had a penchant for mimicry, called up the senator and told him that Governor Horton wanted to see him at the executive residence. The unsuspecting senator immediately got out of bed, dressed, called a cab, and was soon at 2118 West End Avenue. He rang the doorbell and, with some trouble, was able to arouse an aide to the governor.

The aide unsuccessfully tried to persuade the senator that Governor Horton had not summoned him. The senator insisted that the governor be awakened until it dawned on him that Beasley, whom he knew to be a practical jokester, had played a cruel trick on him. The senator and the awakened aide swore vengeance on Beasley but what they did to him is lost to history.[23]

During the political strife in his second term, the deeply religious Horton, whose health was still poor, had even less incentive

Governor Hill McAlister poses with his uniformed staff members. DUB

to socialize at the executive residence. After his second term expired on January 13, 1933, he and Mrs. Horton left Nashville immediately for their farm at Chapel Hill in Marshall County.[24] Governor Horton lived only seventeen months after leaving office. He died on his farm July 2, 1934, after suffering a series of strokes and was buried in the Lone Oak Cemetery in Lewisburg. Later, his remains were moved to Wilhoite Cemetery at Chapel Hill, Tennessee, on the grounds of Henry Horton State Park.

The next governor of Tennessee was Nashville Democrat Hill McAlister, a great-grandson of Governor Aaron Brown and a great-great-grandson of Governor Willie Blount. Hill's wife, Louise Jackson McAlister, had an equally distinguished background. Her father, Howell E. Jackson, had been an associate justice on the United States Supreme Court and her grandfather, General William Giles Harding, was the owner of the famous Belle Meade Plantation. When McAlister was elected gov-

ernor, he and Louise lived in a lovely home at 2507 West End Avenue.[25] As their daughters, Louise and Laura, were already married, the McAlisters lived in the executive residence alone, except for servants, during his four-year term. Mrs. McAlister was an excellent housekeeper and a gracious first lady. During his 1932 gubernatorial campaign, Hill called his wife "the best friend I have in this campaign" and the person "from whom I have received my greatest inspiration."[26]

Once in the executive residence, Mrs. McAlister revived a custom of hosting open houses despite having little state money to spend. A sweet and unselfish person, ever ready to help those in need of assistance, Mrs. McAlister had a hard time dealing with the family members of condemned prisoners. One Sunday, when Governor and Mrs. McAlister were late in life, they had dinner with the author's parents at their home in Nashville. Attending with his parents and brother and sister, the author remembers being fascinated by the fact that Governor McAlister wore a monocle and a hearing aid. Mrs. McAlister, who was the author's

TENNESSEE GOVERNORS AT HOME

great aunt, said that the worst part of being a governor's wife was having to listen to the families of condemned prisoners plead for their loved ones' lives from the front yard of the residence on nights before executions.

During Governor McAlister's first year in office, national Prohibition was still in effect. One day that year, Governor McAlister was entertaining a guest from the Roosevelt administration in the living room at the executive residence. The two men heard a popping noise, which seemed to be coming from the basement. Governor McAlister knew what the noise was but his guest did not. After a moment's hesitation, the governor sheepishly admitted that Mrs. McAlister was in the basement making elderberry wine. She was not arrested.[27]

One of Mrs. McAlister's duties, other than infrequently making moonshine, was to attend an uncomfortably large number of dinners, receptions, and groundbreakings. Her husband was continually invited to attend such events and frequently asked to speak at them. Although his pressing duties as governor during the Depression caused him to regret most such events,

The Hermitage Hotel, Nashville, Tennessee, was often used as election head-quarters during gubernatorial campaigns. RWII

he accepted many. In February 1933, Governor McAlister spoke to the directors of the Southern Newspaper Publishers' Association at the Belle Meade Country Club. Mrs. McAlister was seated with him and James G. Stahlman, publisher of the *Nashville Banner*, at the head table. Later in the month, the McAlisters went to Chattanooga for a Gridiron Dinner. In May, Governor McAlister spoke at Milligan College's commencement exercises. Mrs. McAlister accompanied him by train to Johnson City for the event. In

July, they went to Sewanee, Tennessee, to attend the observance of the fortieth anniversary of the consecration of the Right Reverend Thomas F. Gailor as Episcopal bishop of Tennessee and the twenty-fifth anniversary of his installation as chancellor of the University of the South. The following month, Mrs. McAlister accompanied the governor to Jackson, Tennessee, for the West Tennessee District Fair. Although out-of-town trips normally took Mrs. McAlister away from home overnight, she was pleased to go because it gave her additional, if not undivided, time with her busy husband.[28]

When McAlister ran for a second term in 1934, he stood on his record of having cut costs during the worst year of the Depression. His wife toured the state with him and actively assisted her husband in his successful campaign. Because he advocated further cuts during his second administration, Governor McAlister felt that he must suffer along with state employees. Accordingly, he cut his budget for upkeep of the residence from $35,000 to an astonishingly low $1,000. Hill McAlister loved books and spent many evenings reading in his extensive library. He also found great pleasure in working in his garden and found it a refuge from the pressures of public life.[29] In this avocation, he was often joined by his wife, who was also an enthusiastic gardener and a charter member of the Garden Study Club of Nashville.[30]

After leaving office, Governor McAlister practiced law in Nashville and served as referee in bankruptcy court for the Middle District of Tennessee. One day he was examining a man who was there to present oral evidence on his bankruptcy petition. Governor McAlister asked him, "State your name." The man did not respond and, after McAlister repeated his question several times, the witness said, "Judge, you will have to talk louder. I can't hear a word you say." The governor turned to an assemblage of lawyers present and said, "Boys, pay attention. This is going to be a good show with the hard-of-hearing judge presenting questions to the hard-of-hearing witness." Nashville attorney Charlie Cosner recalled that it was "a good show but that most of the morning was absorbed by the court and the witness trying to understand the questions and answers."[31]

Hill McAlister was succeeded as governor by Gordon Browning, the fifth governor to occupy the executive residence on West End Avenue. The Democrat Browning and his wife, the former Ida Leach, lived there throughout his two-year term. As the mansion was approximately two miles from the State Capitol, Governor Browning did not come home for lunch. He usually ate in the dining rooms of the Hermitage, Andrew Jackson, and Clarkston Hotels. While the West End neighborhood was still attractive, quite a few of the Brownings' neighbors were opting to move to the smog-free suburbs to the southwest of town, particularly near the Belle Meade Golf and Country Club. That the West End neighborhood was changing and neighbors were leaving did not bother either Governor Browning or his quiet and self-effacing wife.

Despite her modesty, Mrs. Browning enjoyed being a member of the Centennial Club of Nashville. In January 1937, Hank Fort was teaching dancing lessons at the club, including a tap dancing class that was so popular it ran an extra month. Most members rode the bus to get to class at the Eighth Avenue South clubhouse. They noticed that Mrs. Browning usually arrived in a chauffeured limousine.[32] Surely, she would have preferred a less pretentious entrance.

When close friends came to 2118 West End Avenue for dinner, they were likely to call Governor Browning by his nickname "Cap." The nickname came from Browning's military days as a member of the famous 114th Field Artillery during

The Centennial Club on Eighth Avenue, Nashville, Tennessee. From *The Centennial Club of Nashville*, 1978.

U.S. soldiers crossing a Stones River bridge during 1943 maneuvers in Middle Tennessee. RWII

World War I. After dinner, Browning sometimes entertained his friends by singing the "Tennessee Waltz," or by reminiscing about the days of his youth in Carroll County, Tennessee.

Gordon Browning was defeated by fellow Democrat Prentice Cooper in the 1938 gubernatorial election. Governor Cooper was a forty-three-year-old lawyer who had graduated from Harvard Law School in 1921 and had served as district attorney general and later in the state senate.[33] Because he was also a bachelor, Cooper invited his mother, Argie Shofner Cooper, to serve as his first lady. She was delighted to accept and did so for the three successive terms he served. Her husband, William Prentice Cooper Sr.,[34] remained at their home at 413 East Lane Street in Shelbyville most of the time but joined his wife and son in Nashville on weekends and other occasions. Argie, who was petite, stylish, and smart, enjoyed her role as first lady and performed it graciously. She was also caring and thoughtful. Andrew and Elizabeth Ewing, who grew up next door on West End Avenue, recalled, in 1998, her hospitality and the Christmas presents she gave them.

Because Governor Cooper opposed a local option liquor bill, which passed over his veto, he felt that it was inappropriate to serve alcoholic beverages in the executive residence. Nevertheless, there were occasions when he had guests who were accustomed to having cocktails before dinner. A friend and cousin, Nashville banker Paul Davis, came up with a solution. He invited Governor Cooper to use his home in Belle Meade whenever such occasions arose, and there were a number of them.

Among the many guests the governor and his mother entertained at the executive residence during World War II were politicians and military officers. Although the house was a handsome one, it was not large enough to accommodate the legislators when they came for dinner, and some of them always had to sit on the stairway. The military officers usually had relationships with one of the new army bases—Camp Campbell, Camp Forrest, or Smyrna Army Air Field—or else were on maneuvers in Tennessee. Governor Cooper had demonstrated foresight in preparing for the war. During a European trip in 1937, he had heard Adolf Hitler speak and was convinced that war was inevitable.[35] Upon assuming office two years later, he persuaded the Tennessee legislature to appropriate a million dollars to a discretionary fund so that the state could purchase land for military bases without delay. During World War II, enlisted men from across Middle Tennessee flocked to Nashville on weekends. Needing places to stay, some soldiers rang the doorbell to the executive residence thinking it was a boardinghouse. Although they were politely turned away, Governor Cooper on occasion entertained troops at the residence.

Governor Prentice Cooper. TSLA

Twice Governor Cooper and his parents watched the University of Tennessee football team play in the Rose Bowl. He entertained the Volunteers following the games. Movie stars Jeanette McDonald and Nelson Eddy became personal friends as a result of those trips to California and were later entertained by Governor Cooper in Nashville. He also hosted Dick Reynolds, president of R. J. Reynolds Tobacco, and his wife, Blitz, at the executive residence. Helen Keller was another memorable guest. She visited the executive residence when she was in Nashville to address the legislature.

Governor Cooper led a very busy life and was not bound by social etiquette. Walter M. Robinson Jr. remembered in 1998 that, as a member of Vanderbilt's Phi Delta Theta Fraternity in 1939 or 1940, he attended a Founder's Day dinner at the Belle Meade Country Club. This was a formal affair to which both active members, alumni, and their guests were invited. At the black-tie event, all the men but one came in tuxedos. Undaunted, Governor Cooper, wearing a gray suit, shook a few hands and left before dinner. A year or two later, Governor Cooper had a date with Huldah Cheek, daughter of Mr. and Mrs. Leslie Cheek, of Nashville. He was to meet Huldah where she was staying, at the home of her close friends Margaret and John Sloan, on Concord Road in Williamson County. Governor Cooper had

At the premiere of *Sergeant York,* Astor Theater, New York City, July 2, 1941. (Left to right): Jesse Lasky, Mrs. Wendell Wilkie, Wendell Wilkie, Mrs. Cooper (governor's mother), Governor Prentice Cooper, and Sgt. Alvin York. TSLA

been with the Sloans the night before at the home of Attie Jarman and Thomas P. Kennedy Jr. on Hillsboro Road. He mistakenly thought that was the Sloans' home. Consequently, the next evening, he went there to meet Huldah. When the butler opened the door, Governor Cooper asked for John Sloan. The butler thought Governor Cooper was John Sloan and invited him to have a seat in the living room. In a few minutes Mr. and Mrs. Kennedy, who were having

dinner, came into the living room expecting to see John Sloan. To their surprise, Governor Cooper was sitting there. The governor was equally surprised to see them. Meanwhile, on Concord Road, Huldah and the Sloans were wondering where the governor was.[36] On another occasion, Governor Cooper invited two Vanderbilt students, Bill and Tom Hudson, to have dinner at the executive residence. The boys, whose mother, the former Violet Hutton, had grown up in

Shelbyville with Cooper, accepted. To reciprocate, they invited Governor Cooper to a dance at the Vanderbilt gymnasium. To their surprise, he showed up. He also had a good time, particularly since the boys introduced him to a number of attractive coeds. Some acquaintances thought that Governor Cooper's manner was stiff. Nevertheless, he enjoyed social occasions, was an engaging dinner partner, and carried on interesting conversations.[37]

Despite early morning smog, which on winter mornings often covered the Vanderbilt area like a blanket, Governor Cooper enjoyed walking in the neighborhood and on the Vanderbilt campus across the street. Normally, he did so in the afternoons or on weekends. One neighborhood boy who noticed him walking along West End Avenue was John L. Seigenthaler, who is currently chairman emeritus of the *Tennessean* and chairman of the Freedom Forum, First Amendment Center at Vanderbilt University. One day, Governor Cooper asked John and a schoolmate at the Cathedral School if they would like to walk with him down to Dan Sanders's pharmacy at the corner of West End and Twenty First Avenues for ice cream cones. Of course, the boys accepted and enjoyed the surprise on Mr. Sanders's face when he saw them enter the drugstore with the governor of Tennessee.

In 1943, Governor Cooper had several dates with Miss Hortense Hayes Powell, a Johnson City native who was taking courses that summer at Vanderbilt. Mrs. Cooper had gotten to know Miss Powell at the 1939–1940 World's Fair in New York where Hortense was a hostess in the Tennessee Building during her summer vacation from Sweet Briar College. Mrs. Cooper and Miss Powell liked each other. When Governor Cooper went to New York for Tennessee Day in August 1940, his mother introduced him to her young friend, Hortense. Governor Cooper was immediately attracted to the vivacious young woman who was twenty years his junior.

The next summer, when Miss Powell was again studying at Vanderbilt, Governor Cooper took her on a boat ride down the Duck River in his native Bedford County. He also invited her on a number of occasions to have

Governors Cooper and Browning (left to right) and three unidentified persons at a veterans celebration. TSLA

dinner in the executive residence. Hortense remembered, in 1998, that dinner was served by the cook; that Mrs. Cooper's portrait, painted by Max Westfield, hung over the dining room fireplace; and that the aqua color of her dress in the portrait was matched in two handsome mantel vases. She also recalled that most of the furniture belonged to the State of Tennessee. Especially notable were the tall, Spanish-style dining room chairs. Governor Cooper owned a large console which had

a record player and a radio. It sat in the upstairs hall sitting room. He also had a Royal Scarlet Macaw parrot named Laura, which often was perched on the front terrace where she could talk to passersby, much to their delight, as she could say about forty words. One evening when Hortense came to the executive residence for dinner, she noticed a pile of paperback novels stacked inside the front door. She wondered "Who in the world is reading these?" She discovered

Governor Jim Nance McCord. TSLA

that Governor Cooper's father loved reading mystery stories.

After three terms as governor, Prentice Cooper was appointed by President Truman as United States ambassador to Peru. He returned to Shelbyville, Tennessee, in 1948 and married Hortense Powell two years later. Their three sons, William P. Cooper III, James H. S. Cooper (United States congressman 1982–1994), and John N. P. Cooper, all live in Nashville. In 1953, Governor Cooper was elected president of the Limited Constitutional Convention. This convention, which amended the state constitution for the first time since 1870, extended the term of the office of the governor from two to four years. For the rest of his life, which ended in 1969, Governor Cooper remained interested in working with his hands,[38] painting with oils,[39] ornithology, and public speaking. His legacy is that of a dedicated lawyer and public servant whose integrity and honesty were never subjects of dispute.

Jim Nance McCord was the last governor to live in the executive residence on West End Avenue. Like Governor Cooper, he was a Democrat and a native Middle Tennessean. Immediately before his election as governor in 1944, he had been United States congressman from Tennessee's Fifth Congressional District. He also was the longtime owner and publisher of the *Marshall Gazette* in Lewisburg and had, for more than a quarter of a century, been both the mayor of Lewisburg and a member of the Marshall County Court. He was also a leader in the cattle and walking horse industries. Such was his love for cattle auctioning once that campaigning for governor and without the knowledge of his campaign staff, he flew to Columbus, Ohio, to conduct a cattle auction for the American Jersey Breeders' Association.[40]

While in office, Governor McCord had to curtail his involvement in the dairy and walking horse industries, but he never lost interest in either, or in activities in Marshall County. During what little spare time he had as governor, he loved to read the *Marshall Gazette* and publications relating to the Tennessee Walking Horse Breeders' Association, which he had helped found, and the American and Tennessee Jersey Breeders' Associations, the latter of which he had served as president. Although he did not have a college education, Governor McCord had gained a love of reading while working in his brother's bookstore as a teenager.[41] He also had a ready wit, an appreciation for the past, and a real liking for people. He once told a reporter that his hobby was "thinking good thoughts about other folks."[42] Generous with his time,

Governor McCord spoke frequently at funerals, graduation exercises, and before civic groups, such as the Nashville Chamber of Commerce.[43]

Mrs. McCord, the former Vera Kercheval of Lewisburg, was interviewed by a Nashville reporter a few months before her move from Marshall County to the executive residence. When asked what she intended to do there, she said, in a beautifully modulated voice, "I just want to stay there and make a home for Mr. McCord. I want my friends to know that the latch-string is always out—our door is never locked here and it never will be in Nashville."[44] She said that she planned to take only her personal belongings and "perhaps a few small pieces" to Nashville and would not move most of her furniture. A person of no pretensions and simple tastes, Mrs. McCord expected to entertain informally as the first lady just as she had done wherever she and Governor McCord had lived. In response to the reporter's question about what she and Governor McCord called each other, Mrs. McCord said that her husband is "Mr. McCord" when she speaks of him to casual acquaintances and

"Jim" at other times. She said he calls her "Honey" most of the time and "Vera" the rest. Mr. McCord explained that he called her "Honey" because "our honeymoon has never ended, because we've always had to depend on each other."[45] On another occasion, he said that Mrs. McCord "is the most radiant bit of sunshine in my life."[46]

Following the precedents set by many of his predecessors, Governor McCord, with Mrs. McCord, traveled extensively across the state to speak at various events. Following Mrs. McCord's death in 1953, Chattanoogans, including Zella Armstrong, recalled the several occasions when Governor and Mrs. McCord led the Grand March for that city's famous Cotton Ball.[47] As first lady of Tennessee, Mrs. McCord also diligently attended events of her own. On October 20, 1948, she was the guest of honor at the annual fall outing of the Ladies' Hermitage Association held at the cabin by the spring at The Hermitage.[48]

Throughout McCord's gubernatorial administration, an exodus of Nashville businessmen and their families from homes in

the Vanderbilt area gradually intensified. Many prominent people like attorney Andrew Ewing, who lived next door to the executive residence at 2114 West End Avenue, were moving to fashionable residential areas in Belle Meade and along Hillsboro Road. Smog, caused by a dependence on soft coal for heat, was a growing problem for Vanderbilt area families. The availability of gasoline after the war made the longer commute from the smog-free suburban areas to offices downtown easier. By 1947, of the twelve houses on the west side of the 2100 block of West End Avenue, one was vacant, another was rented, two had been converted into medical clinics, a fifth was Dr. Roy O. Elam's dental office, the Andrew Ewing house was occupied by a sorority, and the last housed the United States Corps of Engineers.[49] Governor McCord, who was often described as a self-made man, didn't mind living on West End Avenue, despite the smog, the intrusion of commercial establishments, and the fact that his house had leaks that occasionally required buckets to be placed on the floor to catch the water. A plain country Democrat, he just wasn't interested in moving to a more fashionable area. Despite Governor McCord's feelings, the Tennessee legislature in 1947 decreed that the West End property was "no longer suitable for occupancy as a residence for the chief executive of the state." The legislature appropriated $100,000 for a new executive residence with the hope that this amount would be sufficient when added to the proceeds from the sale of the executive residence on West End Avenue. A state committee was appointed to find an appropriate house for Governor and Mrs. McCord and their successors. A member of that committee contacted Earl Woolwine of the Hillsboro-Belle Meade Realty Company to assist in the search. Woolwine put his feelers out. One of the people he talked with was insurance executive Jesse E. Wills, of the National Life and Accident Insurance Company.[50] Woolwine asked Wills if his mother's house, Far Hills, on Curtiswood Lane, might be available. Wills talked with his mother, Mrs. Ridley Wills, about the possibility. They decided she would sell the house to the State of Tennessee for $125,000, provided the state gave her ample time to find a smaller house. Nothing came of the matter, however, as the committee took no further action. Jesse Wills's impression, which was correct, was that Governor and Mrs. McCord were not interested in the property, preferring a smaller house if they moved at all. The state committee chose to be governed by their wishes.

After his defeat for a third term by Gordon Browning, Governor McCord returned to Lewisburg to publish his beloved newspaper and resume, with Mrs. McCord, their civic and church interests.[51] He later served as commissioner of conservation in the cabinet of Governor Frank G. Clement, was a delegate to the Democratic Convention in 1956, and unsuccessfully ran as an independent for governor of Tennessee in 1958. He died on September 2, 1968 in Nashville.[52]

PART TWO

1949–1999

CHAPTER FOUR

FAR HILLS
"A PALATIAL ESTATE"

FORMER GOVERNOR GORDON BROWNING WAS AGAIN ELECTED AS Tennessee's governor in 1948. His statewide vote total was approximately 215,000 while his opponent, incumbent Governor McCord, received just over 160,000 votes. Browning, who was anathema to political boss Edward H. Crump, even carried Shelby County. One morning soon after Browning took office, his good friend, Nashville attorney Jack Norman Sr., was sitting at his breakfast table reading the *Nashville Tennessean*. Mr. Norman usually read the paper each morning cover to cover, including the classified ads. That particular day he noticed that the Ridley Wills home, six miles south of town off Franklin Road, was being offered for sale for $135,000 by realtor C. B. Criddle. The ad, showed a picture of the home describing it as "one of the most outstanding palatial estates in Nashville or even in Tennessee." Norman knew that the state legislature had already decreed that the executive residence on West End Avenue was no longer suitable for the chief executive of the state. He said to himself, "Why not

Far Hills. TSLA

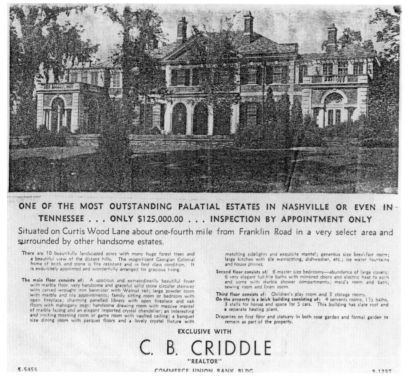

ONE OF THE MOST OUTSTANDING PALATIAL ESTATES IN NASHVILLE OR EVEN IN TENNESSEE . . . ONLY $125,000.00 . . . INSPECTION BY APPOINTMENT ONLY

Situated on Curtis Wood Lane about one-fourth mile from Franklin Road in a very select area and surrounded by other handsome estates.

There are 10 beautifully landscaped acres with many huge forest trees and a beautiful view of the distant hills. The magnificent Georgian Colonial home of brick and stone is fire resistant and in first class condition. It is exquisitely appointed and wonderfully arranged for gracious living.

The main floor consists of: A spacious and extraordinarily beautiful foyer with marble floor, very handsome and graceful solid stone circular stairway with carved wrought iron bannister with Walnut rail; large powder room with marble and tile appointments; family sitting room or bedroom with open fireplace; charming panelled library with open fireplace and oak floors with mahogany pegs; handsome drawing room with massive mantel of marble facing and an elegant imported crystal chandelier; an interesting and inviting morning room or game room with vaulted ceiling; a banquet size dining room with parquet floors and a lovely crystal fixture with

matching sidelights and exquisite mantel; generous size breakfast room; large kitchen with tile wainscoting, dishwasher, etc.; ice water fountains and house phones.

Second floor consists of: 6 master size bedrooms—abundance of large closets; 6 very elegant full tile baths with mirrored doors and electric heat to each and some with marble shower compartments; maid's room and bath; sewing room and linen room.

Third floor consists of: Children's play room and 3 storage rooms.
On the property is a brick building consisting of: 4 servants rooms, 1½ baths, 3 stalls for horses and space for 5 cars. This building has slate roof and a separate heating plant.

Draperies on first floor and statuary in both rose garden and formal garden to remain as part of the property.

EXCLUSIVE WITH

C. B. CRIDDLE
"REALTOR"

5-5455   COMMERCE UNION BANK BLDG.   9-1297

Real estate advertisement featuring the Far Hills property. From a 1948 local publication. RWII

buy Far Hills?" Norman spoke to Governor Browning about the idea and found him as reluctant to pursue the matter as Governor McCord had been. Browning told Norman that "if he spent that kind of money on a mansion, the people of Tennessee would run him out of the state." A mishap in the kitchen of the executive residence on West End Avenue may have made Mrs. Browning more receptive to the idea of a new house than her husband. One day she was cook-ing on a wood-burning stove there when the flue broke. Soot soon covered everything. Mrs. Browning was so exasperated that she said to her husband, "Gordon, you've got to find us a decent place to live."[1]

Despite Governor Browning's reluctance to consider moving to a more expensive house, Norman persisted. He and three other friends of the governor began looking at other homes. The former Paul Davis home on Harding Road interested them but its owners, the Dominican Sisters at St. Cecilia, had no interest in selling. They also looked at Oak Hill, the John Cheek home on Franklin Road. The house they liked best was the handsome Wills mansion, Far Hills.

With the help of House Speaker Jim Cummings, Governor Browning's administrative assistant, Charles Wayland; and Governor Browning's political ally, former state senator William "Rube" McKinney, Norman convinced the governor he should move there. Feeling the purchase would be better accepted by the people of Tennessee if he could get the price down, Governor Browning met personally with Jesse Wills, the owner's son, and talked him into reducing the price by $15,000 and throwing in the furniture as part of the deal.[2] A committee of state officials appointed to buy a new mansion visited Far Hills on November 24 to inspect the property. It met with their approval.[3] Consequently, on January 7, 1949, Jessie Ely (Mrs. Ridley) Wills and Jesse E. Wills, acting as guardian for his father, Ridley Wills, executed a fee-simple deed conveying the eighteen-year-old home to the State of Tennessee for $120,350,

Oak Hill, the John H. Cheek mansion. From *Woodwork,* Clarence Southerland Company, Nashville, Tennessee.

which included furnishings worth $5,350.[4]

National Life vice president Ridley Wills began the construction on the Georgian brick and stone house built for his wife, Jessie, in the fall of 1929. Russell Hart of Hart, Freeland & Roberts was the architect. The principal subcontractors were F. J. Ehrhart, painting;

Fuller-Cunningham Co., tile work; Hebrick and Lawrence, electrical work and plumbing; Nashville Sash and Door Co.; H. E. Parmer Co., roofing and sheet metal work; Clarence Sutherland Co., mill work; and Tanksley-Drumright Cut Stone Company.[5] Concerned about fire safety, Mr. Wills built the house out of reinforced concrete

with masonry walls. The Willses moved in during the summer of 1931. Shortly after this, they hosted a barbecue at Far Hills for all the men who worked on it.[6]

The 1949 advertisements for Far Hills, placed in the *Tennessean* by C. B. Criddle, realtor, described the first floor of the house as having:

Ridley Wills holding his grandson, Ridley Wills II, age sixteen months, October 1935 at Far Hills. RWII

a spacious and extraordinarily beautiful foyer with marble floor; very handsome and graceful solid stone circular stairway with carved wrought iron banister with Walnut rail; large powder room with marble and tile appointments; family sitting room or bedroom with open fireplace; charming paneled library with open fireplace and oak floors with mahogany pegs, handsome drawing room with massive mantel of marble facing and an elegant imported crystal chandelier; an interesting and inviting sun room or game room with vaulted ceiling; a banquet size dining room with parquet floors and a lovely crystal fixture with matching sidelights and exquisite mantel; generous size breakfast room; large kitchen with tile wainscoting, dishwasher, etc.; ice water fountains and house phones.

The front door featured unique peacock door knockers especially ordered by Mr. Wills, who is said to have then asked the manufacturer to destroy the mold.[7] Upstairs, there were "six master bedrooms—abundance of large closets; six very elegant full tile baths with mirrored doors and electric heat to each and some with marble shower compartments; maid's room and bath; sewing room and linen room." On the third floor, there were "a children's play room and three storage rooms."[8]

There was also a brick outbuilding on the property. It consisted of "four servants rooms, one and a half baths, three stalls for horses and space for five cars." The building had a slate roof and a separate heating plant. There was a reflecting pool behind the house. Between it and the garage drive were a long, narrow rock garden and a rose garden with both climbing and bush roses. Along the main driveway up the hill was a strikingly beautiful planting of azaleas. The house cost $152,172.07 to build, not counting the price of the land.[9] During the years that Mrs. Wills lived there, she, her children Jesse Wills and Mamie Craig Clark, their spouses, and an increasing number of grandchildren gathered each Sunday for dinner. There were also elaborate birthday parties for Eleanor Clark, the oldest grandchild.[10]

When the public announcement was made that the W. R. Wills home had been purchased

The main stairwell of Far Hills, home of Mr. and Mrs. W. R. Wills prior to its sale to the state. From *Woodwork*, Clarence Sutherland Company, Nashville, Tennessee.

by the State of Tennessee as a new executive residence, Nashvillians came in droves to see the house. Some of the cars, lined up bumper-to-bumper on narrow Curtiswood Lane, turned around in the driveway of Mr. and Mrs. Andrew B. Benedict Jr., almost directly across the street from the executive residence. Andrew B. "Buddy" Benedict III, then about six, thought the sightseers had mistaken his house for the executive residence. He pulled a little

stool down to the end of the driveway and patiently told the drivers that the governor lived across the street.[11]

Among the first guests to be entertained at Tennessee's beautiful gubernatorial mansion were the wives of the governor's cabinet and the wife of the secretary of state, Mrs. James Cummings, of Woodbury. Mrs. Browning served her visitors refreshments in the morning room and took the ladies on a tour of the house. A

Entrance to the rose garden of Far Hills. From *History of Homes and Gardens of Tennessee*, Parthenon Press, 1936.

staff photographer, Robert C. Holt Jr., accompanied the group on the tour and took photographs which appeared in the *Tennessean's* society section on Sunday, February 27, 1949. The story and photographs were sufficiently newsworthy to occupy an entire page of the newspaper. A month later, Governor and Mrs. Browning hosted the first official reception ever held at the present executive residence. Members of the state legislature and State Capitol news staffers inspected every room in the house from the handsome foyer to the third floor storage rooms.

In the last week of March, at a testimonial dinner held at the Belle Meade Country Club for Nashville songwriter, Mrs. Walter "Hank" Fort, Governor Browning and Nashville mayor, Thomas L. Cummings, were cajoled into appearing before a microphone and singing a duet version of Fort's popular song, "I Didn't Know the Gun Was Loaded." Hank accompanied them on the piano after playing several of her other numbers, including "Put Your Shoes on Lucy," and "Nashville's Such a Friendly Place." The audience, which included Mr. and Mrs.

TENNESSEE GOVERNORS AT HOME

Allen Dobson; Mr. and Mrs. Silliman Evans; Mr. and Mrs. Donald Hart; Mr. and Mrs. Coleman Harwell; Mr. and Mrs. Walter Sharp; Mr. and Mrs. C. Runcie Clements; Hank's mother, Mrs. Cornelius Hankins; and Hank's husband, Walter Fort, loved hearing the renditions.[12]

In the summer, Mrs. Browning invited Mrs. Ridley Wills to come by and see the rose garden, which had been Mrs. Wills's pride and joy. "Mama" Wills, who was then seventy-six years old, was driven to the executive residence by her chauffeur, Lemuel Wilson. She thoroughly enjoyed the visit, during which she walked through the rose and rock gardens and briefly toured the house. Afterward, she told a granddaughter, Eleanor Clark, what a lovely lady Mrs. Browning was and how pleased she was that the Brownings were enjoying Far Hills and taking good care of her roses. Some years later, Mrs. Wills discovered, while driving by the executive residence, that the handsome lead statuary on the lawn had been whitewashed. She was not as pleased with this as she had been with the care of her roses.

In 1979, the old governor's

The lead statuary of deer which graced the lawn of Far Hills was later white-washed by a former first lady. RWII

residence at 2118 West End Avenue was sold to James E. Rice, a local franchisee of Popeye's Famous Fried Chicken. Historic Nashville, Inc. unsuccessfully attempted to block the destruction of the house by taking legal action. However, the court found for the defendant and the house was demolished.[13] The former executive residence was replaced by a Popeye's Famous Fried Chicken outlet. The restaurant did not last and the property will

soon be occupied by Caterpillar Financial Services Corporation.

In an interview given to Louise Davis for an article in the *Nashville Tennessean* of February 17, 1952, Mrs. Browning, the first governor's wife to live in the new executive residence, said that she spent much of her time in the sitting room across the hall from the library where Governor Browning would go through his correspondence in the evenings. During those years, the sitting room fur-

Future Governor Frank G. Clement (left) and Governor Browning (center) march with veterans during the 1949 American Legion Convention in Philadelphia, Pennsylvania. TSLA

niture was a combination of pieces brought from the old executive residence and a few new pieces bought by the state. In the cabinets and on the tables, Mrs. Browning placed glass and china that Mr. Browning collected during the three years he was in Germany after World War II. Mrs. Browning said that most of the silver used in the mansion was their personal property. Their tea service had been made for Governor Browning by a German silversmith. It was copied from the Bremen State silver tea service, Mrs. Browning said.

Upstairs, the Brownings' bedroom was furnished entirely by them. The balance of the upstairs furniture was odds and ends handed down from previous governors. Mrs. Browning commented that "rugs that covered bedroom floors adequately in the governor's residence on West End Avenue looked like scatter rugs" on the floors of the Curtiswood Lane residence. The impression Mrs. Browning gave Louise Davis was that she was satisfied to leave the addition of more elegant furniture to future governors and their wives.

Mrs. Browning told her friends that she considered her house in Huntingdon, Tennessee, to be her real home, and viewed the executive residence as simply a lovely place to stay while her husband was in office. Nevertheless, the Brownings were fine neighbors. When a devastating 1951 ice storm knocked out power all over Nashville, the executive residence escaped the consequences with the use of its auxiliary power system. Governor Browning graciously invited his neighbors, the Andrew Benedicts, to stay with him and Mrs. Browning until power was restored.[14] Because security was minimal during the Browning administration, with an open front gate and only a low stone wall facing Curtiswood Lane, access to the grounds was no problem for neighborhood children, who played on the grounds when they so chose.

Her civic responsibility led Mrs. Browning to open the executive residence to various worthwhile causes. On October 11, 1947, she hosted members of the Nashville Opera Guild for a committee meeting. Present were Mrs. John S. Blunt, Mrs. Thomas Cummings, Mrs. George Hutchison, Mrs. Milton Lewis, Mrs. Robert McGruder, Miss Annie Phillips Ransom, Mrs. Stanley Teachout, and Mrs. Charles Zehnder.[15]

In 1952, while serving his third two-year term, Governor Gordon Browning was eligible for one more consecutive term. He decided to once again became a candidate in the race for governor. His opponents were Frank G. Clement of Dickson, Clifford Allen of Nashville, and Clifford Pierce of Memphis. Clement was victorious in the Democratic primary and went on to easily win the general election.

Twenty-four years later, following Gordon Browning's death in 1976, his friend Aaron Walker said of Browning; "He was a man who walked and sat with the great public men but did not lose the common touch."[16]

CHAPTER FIVE
THE LEAPFROG YEARS

WHEN GOVERNOR AND MRS. FRANK G. CLEMENT FIRST moved into the executive residence in 1953, the public was not interested in spending a lot of money to redecorate it. Mrs. Clement did replace a rose-colored carpet and some draperies.[1] About a year after they moved in, Frank and Lucille Clement's four-year-old son, Frank Jr., bid good-bye to some Dickson County visitors with these words: "Thanks for helping us get this big house to live in."[2] At the time, Frank and Lucille had two other sons, Robert N. "Bob" Clement, the oldest, who was born September 23, 1943, and Gary Clement, the youngest, who was born in 1952. The three Clement boys were the first children to enjoy the new executive residence on Curtiswood Lane. They did not call it that, however, as their father insisted that it be called the governor's residence.[3]

Before being elected governor, Frank Clement was very active in the Methodist Church. Through Methodist contacts, he became a friend of the noted Christian evangelist the Reverend Billy Graham. As a

The Clement family in a formal pose in front of the executive residence. TSLA

61

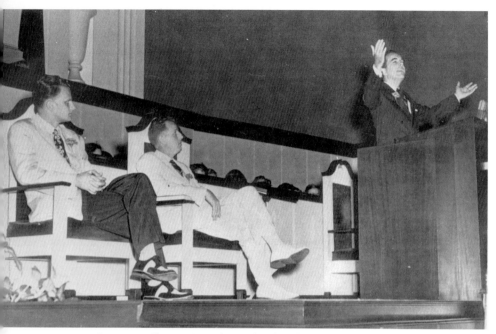

Governor Clement introducing his friend, the Reverend Billy Graham (left), at Birmingham's Central Park Baptist Church, 1953. From the *Nashville Tennessean* library. AP

result of this friendship, Clement met national religious and political leaders who, as friends of Graham, became favorably disposed toward him.[4] Reverend Graham visited the Clements at the Tennessee executive residence on several occasions. On one such visit, he accompanied Governor Clement to the state prison to visit with a condemned prisoner. President Harry Truman also visited the Clements at the executive residence. He did so in

the spring of 1954, after having attended a Ramp Festival in Cosby, Tennessee.[5] Although Mrs. Clement was honored to meet and host Americans as famous as Billy Graham and Harry Truman, she never shared her husband's zest for the public limelight. She did enjoy small dinner parties with friends. Once, prominent Nashville businessman John Sloan and his wife, Margaret, had dinner with the Clements. That evening Mrs.

Sloan had laryngitis and could hardly speak. When Margaret Sloan spoke to her, Mrs. Clement quipped, "With your voice and my looks, I could have been Marilyn Monroe."[6] On another occasion, Mary and Webb Follin Jr. had dinner with the Clements at the executive residence. Mrs. Follin recalled years later how elaborate the fixtures were in the guest bathroom.[7]

Never was Mrs. Clement's husband more in the public eye than in 1956. In January of that year, Buford Ellington and Herbert Walters, state Democratic chairman, touted Governor Clement as a favorite-son candidate for the vice-presidential nomination.[8] He and his supporters made a successful effort for him to be chosen as keynote speaker at the Democratic National Convention held in Chicago that August. The young dynamic Tennessee governor gave an old-fashioned "Cross of Gold" address which he hoped would win the hearts of the conventioneers and gain for him the nomination. The speech, which to many seemed too long, ended with these words, since famous, "Precious Lord, take my hand and lead me on."[9] Clement did not win the vice-presidential nomination, which went to fellow Tennessean, Senator Estes Kefauver. The stress of 1956, which saw Clement travel across the country campaigning for the Democratic ticket that he had hoped to be on, was hard on him. It also took its toll on his wife and their family life. That year and every year her husband was governor, Mrs. Clement had to shoulder most of the responsibilities for rearing their children.

When he was home, Governor Clement was a good but somewhat indulgent father. The children raised chickens, turkeys, and guinea pigs in the backyard and had ponies and horses in the stable. Once, someone gave Bob and Frank Jr. a handsome, green, billy-goat wagon with leather straps. Soon, the boys were parading around the grounds in the cart pulled by two billy goats. That was when Frank discovered that billy goats will eat almost anything, including leather straps. There were also horses and ponies. Bob had a quarter horse named Thunder. Governor Clement gave the children a Shetland pony named Mr. Politics and a walking horse named Go Boy's Play Girl.

Governors Clement and Ellington at inauguration ceremonies during a change of administration. TSLA

Sometime during the fifties, the Clement boys removed all the goldfish and lilies from the three and one-half foot deep reflecting pool so they could swim in it. Their parents went along with the improvement.

Once, Colonel Tom Parker brought up-and-coming rockabilly singer Elvis Presley to the residence for a private concert. Governor Clement arranged for Johnny Bragg and the Prisonaires, a group of blues singers from the state prison, to be there at the same time. Elvis played the piano and sang his song "Hound Dog." The Prisonaires sang the same song to another tune. Bob Clement recalled that Elvis didn't say very much that day and that his father teased Colonel Parker about discovering Elvis. Governor Clement said that since Elvis had earlier worked as a manual laborer for the State Highway Department, he, not Parker, should have discovered him.[10]

The Clement boys quickly grew accustomed to prisoners,

Governor Clement and family with actor Fess Parker, famous for his portrayal of Davy Crockett on television and in films. Copyright *Look Magazine,* from the *Nashville Tennessean* library.

other than entertainers, being at the executive residence. A group of thirteen or so trusties were brought to the residence early each morning and transported back to the state prison after dinner. The oldest Clement son, nine-year-old Bob, thought he was in charge of them and got some "on-the-job training" by supervising their activities. Bob also enjoyed playing basketball and football with the trusties as well as with the highway patrolmen assigned to the residence. He always had difficulty deciding which group he liked best.[11] Frank Clement Jr., who also enjoyed the company of the trusties, recalled in 1998 that some worked outside as gardeners and others inside as houseboys or cooks. Once, a prisoner walked off. Soon, prison guards with bloodhounds were scouring the neighborhood in search of him. Irene Jackson Wills, then a teenager, lived on Norwood Drive, across Franklin Road from the governor's residence. From her house, she saw the bloodhounds and guards searching for the trusty. Irene and her younger brother, Granbery Jackson III, were not allowed to go outside as long as the search lasted. On another occasion, trusties working at the executive residence built a still in the garage and began making illicit whiskey.[12] This escapade did not last very long.

When he got older, Frank Clement Jr. played softball with the trusties and, at least once, ate a cheese and bologna sandwich which a prisoner had brought from the state prison. The prisoner was glad to give his sandwich to Frank because then he had an excuse to go in the kitchen, explain that "Frank Jr. ate my sandwich," and get a hot lunch. Frank Jr. also enjoyed fraternizing with the state troopers. One day when the trooper, who normally sat at a desk in the front hall, was absent, Frank Jr., then about five or six, pulled out of the desk drawer a loaded pistol. He then walked to the kitchen and told everybody to "stick em up," having no idea that the gun was loaded. The frightened employees gently coaxed Frank into putting down the gun. That was one occasion when Governor Clement was not indulgent with his son.[13]

Because there were no gates or fences enclosing the executive residence in the 1950s, neighborhood children felt free to come and go as they pleased. In the summers, Buddy Benedict often rode his bicycle on the executive residence's grounds; he also played horse and other games with his friend, Bob Clement, and the convicts at lunch time. Those were happy years for Bob, Frank Jr., and Gary. When Governor Clement's term expired in 1959, he and his young family moved to a modest three-bedroom house on Curtiswood Circle, not far from the executive residence.[14]

Clement's former campaign manager, Buford Ellington, a native of Holmes County, Mississippi, succeeded him as governor in 1959. After the Ellingtons moved in that January with their eighteen-year-old daughter, Ann, and son John, who was completing his military service in the army at Fort Rucker, Alabama, Mrs. Ellington said, "I nearly walked myself to death get-

Buford Ellington, right, campaigning at the Verona, Tennessee, general store in 1958. TSLA

ting acquainted with the mansion." One of her early decisions was to call the mansion the "executive residence," which it is still called forty years later. Another decision was to put the goldfish and lilies back in the reflecting pool. Governor Ellington said, with tongue in cheek, that Governor Clement built a swimming pool on the property!

During her husband's first term, Mrs. Ellington supervised extensive redecorating and land-

scaping projects. In selecting new draperies, she showed a preference for quiet shades of blue and green in the downstairs reception rooms and upstairs private quarters. In the formal state dining room, she chose sage green satin damask swagged across the windows. She also approved the selection of two handsome breakfronts for the living room. The Volunteer State's first lady also gave attention to the yard. By the summer, roses were blooming

Governor and Mrs. Ellington at his first inauguration, January 1959.
TSLA

behind the goldfish pond. Governor and Mrs. Ellington had undergrowth cleared and magnolia and pine trees planted. They also built flower beds in the recessed garden bordering the lily pool opposite the entrance. The extensive work prompted a gardener to comment, "I just hope that if I stay out here, we won't have another governor that's a farmer."[15]

Mrs. Ellington, who was known for her poise, her unaffectedness, and for being a scratch golfer, soon learned that planning meals and entertaining occupied a whole lot more of her time than golf did. Besides her husband's salary, he received $18,000 in 1961 for maintaining the executive residence. Mrs. Ellington, who had the last say in the operation of the mansion, had the discretionary power to spend the money as she saw fit. Food, she learned, was her biggest item of expense. It came to about $500 per month that year, excluding food for guests, who came often. Mrs. Ellington's guess was that she had about fifty "droppers-in" each month for a meal. In addition to the governor's family and guests, there were nine others to feed—kitchen help, houseboys, and other personnel.[16]

During his first year as governor, Buford Ellington invited a friend, Hugh McDade, a fellow Mississippian then a business executive at the Alcoa Aluminum plant in Maryville, Tennessee, to have breakfast with him at the executive residence. "Mr. Mac," as McDade was called, brought with him his daughter Jane's boyfriend, a nineteen-year-old Vanderbilt student named Lamar Alexander. Just before they entered the mansion, Mr. Mac said to the young Alexander, "I expect you'll live here one day." Once inside at the breakfast table, Lamar Alexander listened as the two men began talking Mississippi, "a language of growling and nudging and elbowing and foot stomping and shuffling around in your chair and table slapping and good-natured cussing and hugely glorified stories about happiness in the rock-hard, barefoot scratching-out days." Living in the executive residence must be like living in a museum, Lamar thought, as a visitor of nineteen.[17]

By the close of her husband's first administration, Mrs. Ellington had gained a great deal of experience in entertaining her husband's friends, such as Mr. Mac, as well as planning diplomatic receptions, open houses, luncheons, and formal dinners for congressmen and national and international officials. In October 1959, a group of educational leaders from Latin America came to the executive residence during their visit to Vanderbilt University. Senator and Mrs. John F. Kennedy spent the night on a campaign swing through Tennessee in September 1960. On that occasion, the Ellingtons had to get a plywood board from a local lumber company to put in the bed the senator slept in. This had been requested because of Senator Kennedy's bad back.

In March 1961, Elvis Presley again visited the residence after being honored at a joint session of the General Assembly for his charitable contributions in Tennessee. Before he received a proclamation from Governor Ellington, Elvis met the governor, the governor's daughter, Ann, and several state officials in a conference room next to the governor's office. Elvis and his road manager, Joe Esposito, were the last to arrive. When he came in, Elvis sat by the governor's pretty daughter, Ann. On the spur of the moment, he invited her to accompany him on a trip to the Tennessee State Prison after the ceremony at the State Capitol. He wanted to see Johnny Bragg, a prisoner whose music he appreciated. Ann agreed to go but had to wait in the car while Elvis went in the prison as she did not have approval to

Governor Ellington's daughter, Ann, with Elvis Presley in 1961. Photo copyright Ann Ellington Wagner Collection. All rights reserved.

accompany him. When Elvis returned, they drove to the executive residence where Elvis prolonged his visit with Ann. The governor, aware that Ann had been entertaining Elvis in the sitting room for some time, hollered to the state trooper on duty, Sergeant Schuller, "tell that hound dog it is time to go." The

trooper dutifully reported to "Miss Ann" exactly what the governor said, and Elvis left.[18] He came back the next weekend, however, while in Nashville for a recording session.

On April 9, 1961, Vice President and Mrs. Lyndon Johnson arrived in Nashville from Geneva, Switzerland, where he participated in nuclear-ban talks and activities surrounding the twelfth anniversary of the North Atlantic Treaty Organization (NATO). In Nashville, Vice President Johnson spoke at a Democratic Jackson Day fund-raising benefit at the State Fairgrounds and threw out the first ball at a Southern League baseball game between the Nashville Vols and Chattanooga Lookouts. The Johnsons spent the night at the executive residence in guest room number one. Vice President Johnson came back to Nashville twice more that fall. On September 3, 1961, he and Mrs. Johnson attended the Tennessee Walking Horse Show in Shelbyville. Later that month, they were in Nashville for the Southern Governors' Conference. The Ellingtons hosted the governors and the Johnsons at a reception at the executive residence.

Bandleader Lawrence Welk was an overnight guest at the executive residence several times, including October 23, 1961, when he was in town for a charity golf event benefiting the Arthritis Foundation. Because there were so many official dinners at the executive residence,

the Ellingtons seldom entertained privately. When they did so, the affairs were usually informal gatherings with such close friends as Joe and Sis Carr and Sam and Marie Hunt.

Because so many citizens of Tennessee were interested in seeing the mansion, Mrs. Ellington established a policy of having people write in advance if they wished to visit the executive residence. They were encouraged to come in groups during the week, thus maintaining family privacy on the weekends. Mrs. Ellington tried to be on hand personally to meet each group and to give them some of the history of the house.[19]

Once during Governor Ellington's first term in office, he participated in a rally in support of the Tennessee Valley Authority (TVA) with Secretary of the Interior Stuart Udall, United States Representative Joe L. Evins, and others on a hot night in Fayetteville, Tennessee. Udall, Evins, and Evins's administrative assistant, Robert N. Moore Jr., had flown from Washington for the rally and later rode back with Ellington to the executive residence, where they spent the night. On reaching the residence,

Governor Ellington took his guests on a tour of the home. At the end of the tour, as the day and long rally had been tiring, he then invited his guests into the kitchen where they assumed they would be offered cocktails. They were wrong! "Almost every night before I go to bed, I come here to the kitchen and have a big bowl of cereal. Won't you please join me?" Ellington said as he poured cornflakes into bowls.[20] On other occasions, Governor Ellington enjoyed having a late evening snack of cornbread crumbled in a glass of cold milk before going to bed. He had a small refrigerator upstairs where he kept the milk and snack food.

As had been the case when Frank Clement was governor, Buford Ellington used trusties from the state prison both inside the executive residence and on the grounds. They were paid about the same amounts they would have earned if they had worked at the penitentiary. They loved having the relative freedom of spending their days at the executive residence. Those who worked outside cleaned the paddock and stable, tended the azaleas, washed the cars of the governor's political supporters, cut the grass, and shot

TENNESSEE GOVERNORS AT HOME

basketball at a hoop Governor Clement had put on one of the doors of the six-car garage. Those who worked inside cleaned the bathrooms, scrubbed the black-and-white marble floor in the foyer, made the beds, and oiled the walnut rail on the carved, wrought-iron banister of the stairway. They also played cards in the basement and cooked and served meals to the governor and his family. One Christmas a young trusty noted that the Christmas tree at the executive residence did not have a star on top. He asked if he could make one. Mrs. Ellington said that she would appreciate it if he did. Using the cardboard liner from one of the governor's dress shirts, the man fashioned a star. He then covered it with aluminum foil and proudly put it on top of the tree. Ann Ellington, who was a student at Middle Tennessee State University (MTSU) during her father's first term as governor, was the executive residence's official tree trimmer. At Christmas 1961, she put up the strings of lights on a flocked tree in the front hall. When questioned about his Christmas gifts that holiday season, Governor Ellington said: "We're not expensive Christmas givers. First of all, we're not rich people. In the second place, we don't think it's just the gift that's the spirit of Christmas." He explained that the cook and the highway patrolmen would be off on Christmas to spend the day with their families and that the Ellingtons would be together as a family, during which time he would reflect on the true meaning of Christmas. On Christmas Eve, the Ellingtons attended a communion service at Glendale United Methodist Church. Governor and Mrs. Ellington hoped to drive down to Mississippi over the holidays to visit his father. If they did so, he said, they would drive through Lewisburg "not stop, just drive through and look around to say 'we've been home.'"[21] The Ellington's son, John Earl, then in the United States Army, celebrated Christmas with his family at the executive residence that year, but daughter Ann recalls that they were unable to get away to Mississippi.

After serving four years as governor, Buford Ellington was not eligible to run again in 1962. When the Ellingtons vacated the executive residence the following January, two of the prized possessions Mrs. Ellington moved out were her sewing machine and upright piano.[22]

Governor Clement decided to run again in 1962. He realized that he needed to do something different to keep people's attention and win the race. Mrs. Clement said "Frank, Bob is in forensics and debate at Hillsboro High School. Let him speak for you." Governor Clement rejected the idea at first and went on with his strenuous campaign schedule, speaking four or five times a day at various courthouses. Soon, he began to lose his voice. This caused him to reconsider Mrs. Clement's suggestion and give Bob a chance. Congressman Bob Clement recalled the campaign:

Dad and I ended up speaking all across the state. He would speak first, then I would speak and spell out all of his accomplishments during his first two terms for whatever county we were in. I would then hand the mike back to him. He would then say to the crowd, 'as a father I'm naturally pleased for the wonderful reception you've given my son, but on August second, don't forget it's ole Frank that's running for governor.' We made history to my knowledge—father and son speaking from the same platforms from Memphis to Mountain City.[23]

Governor Clement was victorious that fall over Mayor Rudy Olgiati of Chattanooga and William Farris of Memphis. Mrs. Clement, who disliked politics even more than she did during her husband's first gubernatorial campaign, and her sons were, nevertheless, pleased to be back in the governor's residence. Gary was a student at Glendale School, Frank Jr. a day student at Battle Ground Academy, while Bob was a freshman at the University of Tennessee.[24]

A memorable day occurred on May 18, 1963, when President John F. Kennedy came to Nashville for a speech at Vanderbilt's Dudley Field and lunch at the executive residence. His visit to Tennessee's executive residence was the first one ever made there by a current president of the United States. Senators Albert Gore Sr. and Estes Kefauver, other members of Tennessee's congressional delegation, Nashville Mayor Beverly Briley, and several presidential staff members, including Pierre Sallinger, had lunch with the Clement family at the governor's residence. In preparation for the visit, Secret Service personnel combed the executive residence and its grounds to insure the safety of the national figures. Frank G. Clement Jr. recalled that Secret Service agents even poured concrete in the holes of trees to preclude the possibility of bombs being placed there. When Governor Clement's neighbor, Sarah "Shug" Benedict, learned about the visit, she got $12 from her husband, Andrew, and bought American flags for the children in the neighborhood to wave when the presidential procession came down Curtiswood Lane. A good number of adults and about thirty children, each holding an American flag, were on hand at the appropriate hour. The procession slowly came down Curtiswood Lane from the south. The children, who were congregated on the west side of the road immediately across from the entrance to the governor's residence, wildly waved their flags. As many as could shook hands with the president, who was riding in his own 1962 Lincoln convertible which had been flown to Nashville.[25]

The president's advance man, Jerry Bruno, worked with Eddie Jones, Governor Clement's press secretary, to make sure that everything went smoothly. Eddie learned that the president favored El Presidente cigars and Heineken beer. The latter caused a problem because Governor and Mrs. Clement had already decided that no alcohol would be served at the luncheon. Eddie solved the dilemma by buying a case of Heineken beer and icing it down in the bathtub in an upstairs guest bathroom. He did so because he knew the president planned to take a shower in the same bathroom upon arriving at the executive residence from Dudley Field. When the president arrived he was discreetly told where the beer was. The plan would have worked perfectly except that before the luncheon one of Tennessee's United States senators used the bathroom and happened to look behind the curtain. Soon, he was back with the other invited guests, beer in hand. The plans for the president to take a shower also went awry. The only person Kennedy wanted with him when he showered and when he changed clothes was Tennessee's governor.

Although Frank Clement was known for his lack of manual dexterity, he insisted on showing the president how the multitude of knobs worked in the shower. By mistake, he turned one on full force dousing the president, who had not yet undressed.[26] Because there were so many guests, the luncheon was held in the master bedroom, where all the furniture had been temporarily removed and replaced with round tables. After the governor's son, Bob, offered a blessing, President Kennedy lifted a glass of ice water and toasted Governor Clement. The lunch included ham, chicken, asparagus, and a desert of strawberry shortcake. After being at the executive residence for only one hour, the president, accompanied by Governor Clement, Mayor Briley, and Senator Kefauver, left in the presidential automobile for nearby John Overton High School, where a military helicopter was waiting to fly him to Muscle Shoals, Alabama. There President Kennedy took part in ceremonies marking the thirtieth anniversary of the signing of the act that created the TVA. As he left the Tennessee executive residence, the president made it a

President John F. Kennedy, Governor Frank Clement (center), and Senator Albert Gore Sr. TSLA

point to thank Lucille Clement for her gracious Southern hospitality.[27]

In December, Governor and Mrs. Clement decided to let son Gary celebrate New Year's Eve with a party in the executive residence. What they did not count on was a winter storm that hit Nashville that night. Heavy snow and deteriorating road conditions influenced the Clements to arrange for the boys to spend the night on cots set up on the third floor and for the girls to sleep in the bedrooms on the second floor. About eleven that night, Governor Clement called Eddie

Jones, his press secretary, and asked him if he thought having the teenagers spend the night was a good idea. Jones deadpanned, "You won't know for nine months." There was a detectable pause on Clement's end of the connection followed by some cursing. Governor and Mrs. Clement followed through with their plans, after having a state trooper inform the parents, but did not sleep well.[28] On earlier Christmases, Governor Clement had been known to pile his boys in the family car and deliver Christmas baskets to Nashville's needy.

In 1965, the Vanderbilt basketball team won the Southeastern Conference championship. To honor the accomplishment, Governor and Mrs. Clement invited the players; their coaches, Roy Skinner and Don Knodel; trainer, Joe Worden; and team manager, John Tarpley, to the executive residence for a reception. It was a toss-up as to who had the most fun—Clyde Lee, Snake Grace, John Ed Miller, Keith Thomas, Wayne Taylor, Wayne Calvert, and their teammates or Governor and Mrs. Clement and their sons, the three of whom shot a few hoops with the players on the Clements' outside court.

Governor Clement was also a huge fan of country music and was a personal friend to many country music stars and entertainers, including Eddie Arnold, the Carter family, John and June Carter Cash, Minnie Pearl, Dinah Shore, and Tennessee Ernie Ford. On many occasions, friends from the country music industry came to the executive residence both to entertain and to be entertained.

During his second term, Governor Clement's father-in-law, Nelson Christianson, who lived in Houston County, was suffering from prostate cancer. Lucille and Frank invited him to stay with them as the executive residence would be more convenient to the medical treatment he needed in Nashville. On Christmas Day, the Clements felt that Mr. Christianson needed the attention of a physician, so Governor Clement called his personal urologist, Dr. Thomas E. Nesbitt, and asked him to come by. Dr. Nesbitt did so and quickly found the elderly gentleman to be in a stable condition. While there, Governor Clement asked Tom to stay a while and listen to Lucille play the white organ Frank had given her for Christmas. Dr. Nesbitt did so for about an hour. While sitting in the executive residence listening to Lucille play he wondered what he was doing there instead of being home with his own family.[29]

In 1966, Bob Clement became the first child of a governor to be married in the executive residence on Curtiswood Lane. He and Marilyn Wyms took their marriage vows there a year before his father left office and three years before Governor Clement's tragic death in an automobile accident on November 4, 1969.

During the Clements' last year in the executive residence, Frank Gorrell and Jared Maddux were running against each other for the positions of speaker of the senate and lieutenant governor. The *Tennessean* backed Gorrell while the governor was for Maddux. One night, when Frank Clement Jr. drove home, he found the front entrance to the executive residence blocked by the automobiles of members of the staff of the *Tennessean*. They were trying to identify any state senators who might be visiting the governor that evening on behalf of Jared Maddux. Only after explaining that he lived there was the increasingly agitated teenager able to get the cars moved so that he could proceed up the driveway.[30]

On his last day in office, Governor Clement asked his personal secretary, Mary Smith, to bring to the executive residence the clemency papers for Johnny Bragg, a convicted felon who had long worked for Governor and Mrs. Clement at the executive residence and gained their confidence. Already, Governor Clement had the district attorney's approval to pardon Bragg, whose musical group, the Prisonaires, had performed a number of times for the

Clements. The governor pardoned Bragg in an emotional scene in which Bragg, overcome with emotion, promised the governor that he would henceforth be a model citizen. He kept that promise.[31]

Buford Ellington was swept into office as governor for a second time in November 1966 when he carried every county in the state. When Mrs. Ellington moved back into the executive residence, she brought with her the sewing machine and upright piano she had moved out four years earlier.[32] Feeling that "since the house was often used for public functions, it should be something the people of Tennessee could be proud of," she had the house cleaned and repainted. She also installed some new draperies and carpets in the front hall, including a handsome area rug with the Tennessee State Seal on it. She additionally acquired two Louis XIV vases for the dining room, several paintings, and a gilded mirror eight feet tall.[33] The Ellingtons' daughter, Ann, an artist, tackled the restoration of a mural on the wall beside the front stairway landing.

On March 14, 1967, Mrs. Lyndon Johnson arrived in Nashville. At the Nashville Municipal Airport to meet the first lady that evening were many private citizens, as well as a number of Tennessee dignitaries, including Governor and Mrs. Ellington, their daughter and son-in-law, Ann and Timothy Wagner, and the Wagners' little daughter, Malinda. After speaking to some people in the crowd and to the press, Mrs. Johnson climbed into a car with the Ellingtons and rode in a motorcade to the executive residence, where she was an overnight guest.[34] President Johnson surprised his wife and the Ellingtons by flying in the next day. Theirs was the second presidential visit in four years. On Andrew Jackson's two-hundredth birthday, the Ellingtons accompanied the presidential party to The Hermitage.[35] President and Mrs. Johnson then went to Columbia, Tennessee to visit the James K. Polk home and to dedicate Columbia State Community College. Mrs. Ellington stayed at the executive residence to oversee preparations for the reception and dinner she and Governor Ellington hosted for the Johnsons and twelve newspaper publishers that evening. Following the dinner, the Johnsons flew back to

Governor Buford Ellington. TSLA

Washington. One of the Nashville ladies who had an opportunity to chat with the president earlier in the day said, "He puts you so much at ease. You had the feeling he would honestly love to stay and keep on talking. I wanted to tell him he'd better hurry or he'd be late for his next reception."[36]

One Nashvillian almost got in trouble as a result of President Johnson's visit. Dave Alexander Jr., who was then a sophomore at Nashville's Montgomery Bell

Governor and Mrs. Buford Ellington. Photo copyright Ann Ellington Wagner Collection. All rights reserved.

Academy, lived on North Curtiswood Lane, behind the executive residence. He had no idea the president of the United States was next door the afternoon of the president's visit. Dave, who had just planted a vegetable garden in his backyard, was fearful that the squirrels would eat his young vegetables.

He addressed the problem by shooting a squirrel with his shotgun. A state trooper heard the shot and quickly arrived on the scene. He asked Dave what in the world he was doing. Dave said that he had simply shot a "varmit." The trooper told the boy to go in the house and not come back outside because President Lyndon Johnson was next door.[37]

Back in 1958, when he was first elected governor, Buford Ellington, a former commissioner of agriculture, had temporarily set up offices to organize his administration in Brentwood Hall, the former home of Rogers Caldwell. Following his inauguration, Ellington decided against selling the estate, which the state had acquired in 1957, and moved some agricultural offices from downtown to the 207-acre site. Brentwood Hall was renamed Ellington Agricultural Center by a resolution of the legislature in 1961, when Governor Frank Clement moved the headquarters of the Tennessee Department of Agriculture there. Governor Ellington was fond of the center.[38] Accordingly, during his second administration, he enjoyed walking there on the weekends with his

first grandchild, Malinda Wagner, born in 1965 to Ann and Tim Wagner, who had married two years earlier following Ann's graduation from MTSU.

The Ellington family enjoyed animals and, as Ann said in 1998, had "lots of dogs and cats" while living in the executive residence. It was also natural for a governor, who had lived in Marshall County, the home of the Tennessee Walking Horse Breeders' Association, to have a Tennessee walker. The Ellingtons kept one in the stable at the executive residence.

Martin Luther King's assassination in Memphis on April 4, 1968, pointed out the need for greater security at state properties. After Winfield Dunn's election but before Governor Ellington left office, the governor spoke to Dr. Dunn about the idea of building a fence around the executive residence with an electronically controlled gate. "You have two little girls, don't you?" Governor Ellington asked. Dr. Dunn said he did. The governor then said he had been thinking about building a fence around the executive residence because of the death threats he received after Martin Luther King's murder and because of the unrest that occurred in Nashville as an aftermath of the assassination. He asked Dr. Dunn what he thought. Dr. Dunn said that he really had not considered the idea but that he had great respect for the governor's judgment and would defer to his opinion. With this approval, Governor Ellington had the state architect draw up plans and show them to Dr. and Mrs. Dunn for their approval. The security fence and gate, which Betty Dunn helped design, were completed during the first year of the Dunn administration.

As the end of 1970 got closer, the Ellingtons thought of how they might make life easier for Governor and Mrs. Dunn. They decided that possibly the best way they could help would be to move out of the executive residence a week early so the Dunns would have a little extra time to move their family from Memphis to their new home in Nashville. The Ellingtons did this. When the Dunn family got to Nashville, the governor invited them to visit him at his office at the State Capitol. There, standing before a portrait of Andrew Jackson, Governor Ellington said to Winfield and Betty Dunn, "We have been here eight years and I want to give you some advice. 'Don't change when you come in so you won't have to change when you go out.'" This was wise counsel which the Dunns took to heart. After reflecting on the courtesies shown them by Governor and Mrs. Ellington, Betty Dunn said, in 1998, that "they were sweet and wonderful to us."

Governor Ellington died suddenly while playing golf in Florida in 1972. His body was flown back to Tennessee for burial at Lone Oak Cemetery in Lewisburg, where the remains of two earlier Tennessee governors, Henry Horton and Jim Nance McCord, had been buried in 1934 and 1968 respectively.

CHAPTER SIX
THE FIRST REPUBLICAN GOVERNOR IN FIFTY YEARS

THE SECOND WEEK OF JANUARY 1971, WINFIELD DUNN, A Memphis dentist; his wife, Betty; their three children, Chuck, Gayle, and Julie; and their wirehaired terrier, Christy, moved into the executive residence on what was then called South Curtiswood Lane. Chuck was then a student at Washington and Lee. Gayle was a fourteen-year-old high school student, while Julie, ten, was in elementary school. When she had time to think about something other than unpacking and getting her daughters into new schools, Betty Dunn reflected on an impression formed when she visited the executive residence earlier. Except for the handsome V'Soske hooked carpet in the entrance hall with the Great Seal of the State of Tennessee indelibly woven in it, Betty saw nothing in the house that said that you were in the residence of the governor of Tennessee. She was mulling over a series of actions to address the shortcoming.

Soon after her husband's election, Mrs. Dunn enjoyed visits to the governors' residences in Frankfort, Kentucky, and Richmond, Virginia, to get

Governor Winfield Dunn and family (left to right): Chuck, Betty, Julie, Governor Dunn, and Gayle. WD

ABOVE: Following the inauguration of Governor Dunn, a lengthy line of well-wishers formed outside the executive residence. From the *Nashville Tennessean*, January 18, 1971.

TOP: The executive residence December 1972. TSLA

ideas on how she might improve the Tennessee executive residence. Betty was impressed that both houses were periodically open to the public and that the public rooms in each were furnished with books, furniture, paintings, portraits, and silver that reflected the states' heritage and brought a sense of history to the executive residences. She knew then what might be done for Tennessee's executive residence.

Before moving to Nashville, Mrs. Dunn called Roupen M. Gulbenk, a Nashville art connoisseur and dealer, identified herself as the future governor's wife, and asked for his and his wife's help in planning a series of inaugural parties at the governor's residence. The Gulbenks were glad to help but were soon horrified to find that the executive residence had no appropriate silver, linen, or crystal for the forthcoming receptions. So they scurried around and borrowed whatever they needed to insure that the parties were elegant. Mrs. Gulbenk also decorated the executive residence for the several inaugural parties. The lack of silver, linen, and crystal made the point clear to Betty Dunn that much needed to be done.

Mrs. Dunn knew that the Tennessee executive residence's furnishings and decorations were "nice and neat" but not reflective of the dignity of the magnificent home that her family now occupied but which really belonged to the people of Tennessee. She moved on two fronts. Gathering her nerve and "shaking like a leaf," she appeared before the State Building Commission in early 1971 to ask for state funds to replace worn-out fabrics, carpets, and materials at the executive residence. Mrs. Dunn recalled in 1998 that, as she sat before Jim McKinney, William R. Snodgrass, and John S. Wilder, to plead her case, they were seated above her, making them appear even more formidable than they already were. As it turned out, they wanted to help and approved an expenditure of $92,000 on the executive residence.

One change cost the state nothing. When the Dunns moved into the executive residence they noticed that a state trooper was routinely seated in a chair behind a desk in the entrance hall to the left of the front door and immediately in front of the only downstairs bathroom. They also noticed that the desk had a gold telephone on it, which seemed a little ostentatious. The Dunns decided to let the issue of the gold telephone slide but to move the command station to the other side of the front hall beyond the door to the state dining room. That way, family members and guests would not feel uncomfortable using the bathroom. The move was made with no fanfare and no fuss. About the same time, a security system was installed at the troopers' station.

Soon after her husband became governor, Mrs. Dunn began having public receptions at the executive residence, following the pattern of those she learned about in Frankfort and Richmond.[1] By the following September, the residence was regularly open for two hours each Tuesday and Thursday afternoon with docents, provided by various women's organizations, who guided the visitors.

Betty Dunn knew that acquiring the proper china, silver, and crystal, as well as books, works of art, and antique furniture produced by Tennessee artists, authors, and craftsmen, would require help from the private sector. "There have been so many

Governor Winfield Dunn. TSLA

fine artists throughout the state," she said. "It has been my hope that we could work out a program to feature the works of different ones in the area." She already knew whom to ask for assistance. Roupen and Mary Sue Gulbenk had already proved themselves by planning and decorating for the successful inaugural receptions. The Dunns, accordingly, asked Roupen if he would

ABOVE: Mrs. Dunn with Andrew Jackson portrait. TSLA

RIGHT: First Lady Betty Dunn happily receives silver service for the executive residence. TSLA

chair a nonprofit organization to encourage Tennesseans to make suitable gifts or loans to the executive residence. He accepted. On May 19, 1971, the Tennessee Executive Residence Preservation Foundation, Inc. was created with sixteen members.[2] The foundation's main purpose was to acquire furnishings and fixtures, works of art, and other articles which are either of Tennessee origin or are of artistic interest to Tennesseans.

The first item acquired, even before the foundation was established, was an oil portrait of General Andrew Jackson by Samuel Waldo. Mr. Gulbenk learned that the portrait, which had been owned by the Chaille family of New Orleans, was being offered for sale by the C. G. Sloan Gallery of Washington, D.C. He interested the Justin and Valere Potter Foundation of Nashville in buying the painting and loaning it to the executive residence. The foundation agreed to do so and authorized Mrs. Dunn to attend the auction and bid on the painting. She did this in February 1971 and bought the portrait, which was painted from life between 1817 and 1819, for $52,000. The portrait, which the Potter Foundation gave to the State of Tennessee in 1996, continues to hang over the mantelpiece in the drawing room of the executive residence.[3]

In February 1971, Owen N. Meredith, director of the Tennessee State Museum, made available to Mrs. Dunn for the executive residence a treasured silver set from the museum's collection. A fifteen-gallon Gorham silver bowl and cups from the decommissioned battleship USS

Tennessee were soon delivered to the executive residence, where they were placed on the sideboard in the dining room and where they have ever since been used at official teas and receptions.[4] Governor and Mrs. Dunn wanted to personally participate in the restoration effort. Accordingly, they acquired a map of Tennessee, dated 1795, to hang in the executive residence.

One of the Tennessee Executive Residence Preservation Foundation's first acquisitions was a handsome mahogany Chippendale secretary given by prominent Memphis businessmen Abe Plough, S. L. Kopald, and Kemmons Wilson. The secretary, which was placed in the parlor, was once the property of President Woodrow Wilson and had been handed down in his family. Another early purchase, made possible through the generosity of *Nashville Banner* publisher Irby Simpkins and board chairman Brownlee O. Currey Jr., was an exceptionally fine Federal, inlaid hunt board. At the same time, the Sultzberger Foundation of Chattanooga contributed a Federal-period mirror to complement the hunt board. The mirror, which had hung over

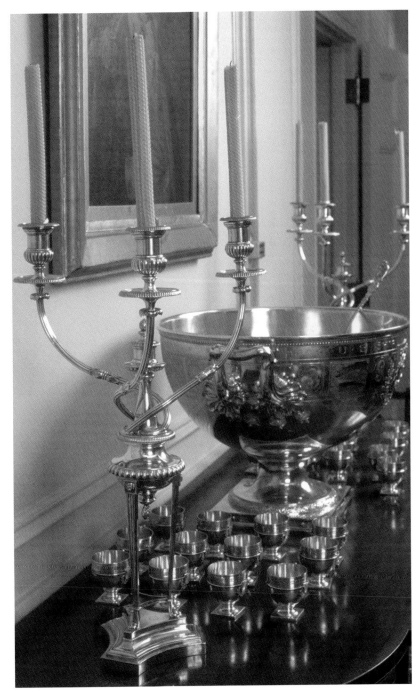

USS *Tennessee* silver service. TPS

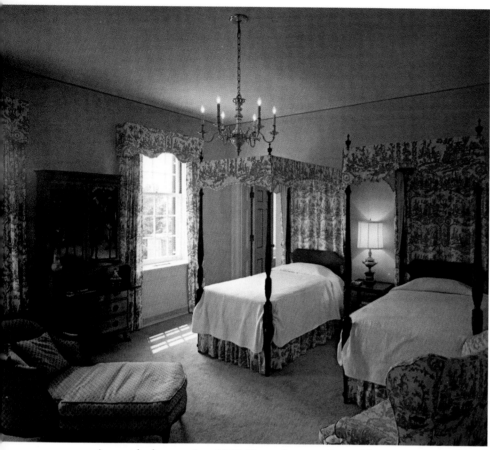

A guest bedroom, circa 1975. From the executive residence guidebook.

the hunt board in a previous collection, was hung in its accustomed position at the executive residence. Another outstanding piece contributed during the foundation's first year was a breakfront given by Mr. and Mrs. Jack Massey of Nashville. Mr. and Mrs. H. Clay Johnson, of Lookout Mountain, gave an aged grandfather clock made by James Cary of Brunswick, Maine, in 1780. The clock was placed on the landing of the spiral stairway in the entrance hall. The National Life and Accident Insurance Company contributed a complete set of flat silver to the state for the executive residence, while Third National Bank contributed a set of porcelain embossed with the state seal.

In 1972, Mr. and Mrs. Sam M. Fleming, Mr. and Mrs. Ernest Moench, and Mrs. Hugh Stallworth, all of Nashville, contributed a 1790-period New York Hepplewhite sideboard to the executive residence. The piece had once been in the New York home of Robert R. Livingston, the United States ambassador to France under President Thomas Jefferson. According to tradition, the sideboard was there during negotiations for the purchase of the Louisiana Territory from France.[5]

If new ground was broken in the areas of opening the executive residence to the public and furnishing the home with items reflective of the heritage of the state, other traditions remained unchanged. Governor Dunn continued having trusties from the Tennessee State Prison work at the executive residence, both in the house and on the grounds.

One day, after returning to the executive residence unexpectedly early, Mrs. Dunn went upstairs and began working at the desk in her office. In the adjacent hall there is now, and was then, a back stairway leading downstairs to the hall outside the kitchen. The upstairs door to the stairway automatically locked when closed. Earlier that day, when Julie Dunn had gone down the stairs, she had inadvertently left the door ajar. One of the trusties noticed this. Not realizing that Mrs. Dunn was home, he went up the stairs and took two bottles of champagne from the refrigerator in the hall. Mrs. Dunn heard him. She got up from her chair and walked into the hall, where she saw the trusty, whom she liked very much, with the two champagne bottles under his arm. Mrs. Dunn told him to put them back as they were not his. He did so and left. Mrs. Dunn did not mention the incident to anyone that day. That night, however, she could not sleep, worrying about the incident. Accordingly, she got up and went downstairs and told the state trooper, Wayne Steele, what happened. He immediately said that the trusty could never come back to the executive residence. He explained that the man, whom Mrs. Dunn had found to be an excellent house cleaner, had been convicted of murder, a crime he had committed while drunk.[6] Possibly influenced by this incident, the Dunns considered discontinuing the system of having state prison trusties work at the executive residence.

However, as state funds to maintain the residence were scarce, they felt they could not afford to make the change. Besides, most of the trusties never betrayed the trust given them at the executive residence.[7]

Continually aware that her husband was the first Republican governor in fifty years and that, to be successful, he had to work harmoniously with a Democratic controlled General Assembly, Betty Dunn set out to win the friendship and cooperation of the state's legislators. During Governor Dunn's first year in office, she sent formal invitations to all of the state senators and members of the Tennessee House of Representatives, inviting them and their spouses to one of two dinners to be held at the executive residence, each at 6:30 P.M. To accommodate the large number of guests, Mrs. Dunn had a tent erected. After dinner each evening, the lawmakers were treated to a fabulous show featuring Grand Ole Opry stars and other famous entertainers. The only hitch Mrs. Dunn could recall was that on the afternoon of the first party some legislators and their wives arrived a few minutes after 5:00 P.M. Mrs. Dunn later

Governor and Mrs. Dunn. TSLA

learned that they had been accustomed to attending barbecues given at the executive residence by Governor and Mrs. Ellington which did start at 5:00 P.M.

One of the more formal dinner parties at the executive residence during the Dunn years was for the board of directors of General Motors. Victor Johnson, a Nashville industrialist and a devoted member of the board of trust of Meharry Medical College, was indirectly responsible for the affair. He encouraged the board to meet in Nashville in hopes that George Moore, executive vice president of General Motors, and other board members might be

World famous Grand Ole Opry star Minnie Pearl and her husband, Henry Cannon, were neighbors of the executive residence on Curtiswood Lane, and frequent guests of several governors. RWII

Governor and Mrs. Nelson D. Rockefeller of New York were overnight guests of the Dunns. Mr. Rockefeller, who taught a Sunday school class, came to speak to the first prayer breakfast held by Governor Dunn. He had been invited to speak when the two men met in New York. Before the Rockefellers arrived, their advance man had requested that a board be put in Governor Rockefeller's bed at the executive residence and that he be served dubonnet with a twist of lemon at the reception given in his honor on the evening of their arrival. The Dunns willingly complied with both requests. Governor and Mrs. Rockefeller enjoyed the reception at which they were treated to a musical review by Opryland singers. Mrs. Rockefeller, whose nickname was "Happy," left Nashville impressed with the Southern hospitality she and her famous husband received.[8]

Other guests of the Dunns at the residence were Governor Jack Williams of Arizona, native-Tennessean Dinah Shore, Vice President Spiro Agnew, and movie star Burt Reynolds. The latter, while a house guest of Mr. and Mrs. Buddy Killen, came to a country supper at the Tennessee executive residence on a Sunday evening. Also in attendance that evening were the Killens and executive residence next-door neighbors Henry and Sarah (Minnie Pearl) Cannon. The group played tennis, watched an NFL game on television, and sang "old country songs," led by Minnie Pearl at the piano. Reynolds was so taken by the evening that he later hosted a two-hour national television show from the executive residence on NBC. Betty Dunn recalled in 1998 how much planning went into the show, how extensive the cabling was, and how good the presentation was. A parade of stars performed, including Charlie Rich, Dinah Shore, and Dolly Parton. Governor Dunn recalled that the State of Tennessee provided Reynolds its King Air aircraft so he could be filmed landing at Nashville's airport in a State of Tennessee airplane.

One of the many times close friends came to the executive residence was on July 1, 1971, when First Lady Betty Dunn had a birthday party for her forty-four-year-old husband. In June 1998 she wrote:

sufficiently impressed with the mission of Meharry that they would choose to support the school financially. The Tennessee Department of Economic Development served as the official sponsor of the dinner.

We love celebrating birthdays, so when Winfield had his "first" birthday there we decided to have a beautiful dinner party in the State Dining Room and invite our close friends, among them a future governor and first lady, Lamar and Honey Alexander. We set that long table with a lovely tablecloth that came almost to the floor, china, crystal, etc. and, of course, planned for a birthday cake to be brought out at the end of dinner. It was fun to be with our friends but I noticed an unusual amount of giggling and knowing glances among our guests. I had no idea at the time that our youngest daughter, Julie, then ten, was under the table 'tweaking' our guests toes and whispering that they should not give her away. Can you imagine Winfield's surprise when, ready to blow out the candles, Julie jumps out from under the table singing 'Happy birthday, daddy!'[9]

Governor and Mrs. Dunn at home in Nashville. WD

Mrs. Dunn also recalled in 1998 that entertaining in the executive residence was possible because of the able assistance of her staff, including that of her residential director, Virginia Smartt, who planned and organized most of the special events.

Of the vast number of nonprofit organizations to visit the executive residence during her husband's administration, Betty Dunn remembered a visit sponsored by the Easter Seal Society of Tennessee as perhaps the most meaningful. Asked by the director of the Easter Seal Camp if she might bring some disabled children to tour the executive residence, Mrs. Dunn naturally said yes. When the children, some on crutches, some in wheelchairs, and one carried because he was missing arms and legs, came out of the vans, Mrs. Dunn realized that the visit would be an emotional one. She put on her best smile and invited them in the house. The children were wide-eyed with excitement. Among their questions was whether or not they might meet Minnie Pearl, whom some knew to be a next-door neighbor. Betty Dunn whispered to a state trooper to call Sarah Cannon to see if she might possibly come over for a few minutes. Luckily, she was at home. The gracious First Lady of Country Music assented and in a few minutes arrived to greet the children, who were by then seated under a tent in the front yard enjoying juice and cookies. Years later, Betty Dunn recalled what happened next:

After entertaining them for a few minutes with funny stories about Grinder's Switch, Mrs. Cannon asked the children to give her a gift. A look of wonderment came over their faces. She said that she knew that they had been to camp and had learned some songs and would they share some of them

with us. Needless to say they proudly sang their little hearts out, happily knowing that they had given something of themselves to Minnie and me.[10]

As have other first ladies, Betty Dunn did her best to make the years her daughters lived at the executive residence as normal as possible. Because Chuck, nineteen, was already a student at Washington and Lee, he needed less protection. Chuck was sensitive to his situation, however. When Robert McDowell gave him a construction job the first year the Dunns were in Nashville, Chuck got through the summer without any of his co-workers knowing he was the son of the governor of Tennessee. When asked what his father did, Chuck simply said "he works for the state." Chuck's sister, Gayle, enrolled at Harpeth Hall in midyear as a ninth grader, while Julie, the youngest, entered Oak Hill as a fourth grader.

Like most children, the Dunn girls enjoyed listening to music on tapes and radios. One day, Governor Dunn received a politely worded letter from a neighbor complaining about the music coming from the executive resi-

dence. She wrote that the noise was so loud it came through her closed windows and doors. Governor and Mrs. Dunn were never sure whether the music came from their daughters' rooms or from the garage where the prisoners enjoyed listening to loud music while washing automobiles and performing other chores. Regardless, Julie was sensitive to the family's need to be good neighbors. Once she walked to every neighbor's house to explain that she was planning to have a party at the executive residence on the following weekend and to promise her neighbors that she and her friends would "not be wild" and that the party would end at 10:00 P.M. The neighbors were impressed. Several wrote notes or called Betty Dunn to compliment her daughter.

While living at the executive residence, the Dunn girls had a Tennessee walking horse, a gift from the Tennessee Walking Horse Association, and a calf named Buckalena, another gift to Governor Dunn. The animals shared a stall in the garage, which worked pretty well because Buckalena thought she was a horse anyway. The horse was gentle with the calf even though the latter had a very bad habit of nibbling on the horse's tail. While living at the executive residence, the Dunn's twelve-year-old wirehaired terrier, Christy, died. She was buried in the garden with appropriate ceremonies. Governor Dunn was offered quite a few gifts while he was governor, including a limousine and an offer to build a swimming pool. He politely declined these two, although a pool would be built at the executive residence a few years later during Lamar Alexander's tenure as governor.

In 1974, shortly before Governor Dunn left office, the Tennessee General Assembly, in a joint session, paid tribute to Mrs. Dunn. Cumberland University singers performed, senior state officials praised her, and she was presented with a sterling silver tray and silver service in recognition for her hospitality to them and her service as a gracious and caring first lady of the state. Mrs. Dunn was also honored by having the Betty Dunn Nature Center at Fall Creek Falls State Park named in her honor.

When the time came for the Dunns to leave South Curtiswood Lane, Governor and Mrs. Dunn recalled the courtesy extended them by Governor and Mrs. Ellington in moving out a week early. They did the same for the succeeding first family, the Ray Blantons.

In the years following his service as the state's chief executive, Governor Dunn has remained engaged in a varied business career. Considering his professional background in dentistry, it is not surprising that his interests have been directed toward health-related matters. He continues to be actively involved, currently as vice chairman of Network Health Services, a medical information management company located in Nashville.

CHAPTER SEVEN
A WEST TENNESSEE DEMOCRAT ARRIVES

I N 1974, FORTY-FOUR-YEAR-OLD DEMOCRAT RAY BLANTON OF Adamsville won the governorship, defeating Lamar Alexander, who had successfully managed Governor Dunn's Republican campaign in 1970. When he was inaugurated in January 1975, the new governor was almost unknown to Nashville's business leadership. He was well-known otherwise, having served three terms in the U.S. House of Representatives before losing a U.S. Senate race in 1972 to incumbent Republican Senator Howard Baker. Ray Blanton, his wife, Betty Littlefield Blanton, and their two sons, twenty-one-year-old David and nine-year-old Paul, soon moved into the executive residence. An older daughter, Debbie Blanton Flack, had already married and was living in Gallatin with her husband, Lewis D. Flack III. The Blanton household also included twenty-two staff members—a chef, Charles French, whose salary was $14,000 a year; two administrative assistants; a gardener; eight inmates who worked inside; and ten inmates who worked on the grounds.[1] Having inmates work at the executive residence was a

Governor Blanton hosts a holiday party for his staff and their families at the executive residence in 1978. TPS

89

Governor Ray Blanton. TSLA

practice that Governor Frank Clement had started. Blanton continued the practice because it saved the state a considerable amount of money. Soon he developed the habit of introducing the trusties who served at dinner parties held at the executive residence. At a certain point during the meal, on a signal from the governor, they would line up behind his chair after which each man would step forward, in turn, and recite his name, age, home-

town, the nature of his crime, and his sentence. Some guests were uncomfortable with this practice. Governor Blanton never was. Lamar Alexander witnessed such a recitation, and when he visited the executive residence following his election in 1978, he said to Governor Blanton, "You didn't have to do that." The governor smiled and responded, "Aw, they like it."[2] Mrs. Blanton, who was always a gracious hostess and discreet wife, did not enjoy the recitals and would have preferred that her husband not comment at all about the waiters.[3] Before dinner parties, Governor Blanton often took his guests on a tour of the residence. Sometimes he would mention that he intended to rewrite its official history because the version adopted during the Dunn administration was partial to the Republicans. He also was prone to pause by the portrait of Andrew Jackson and comment that "Old Hickory" was someone he greatly admired.

During their first Christmas season in the executive residence, the Blantons held a reception for members of his cabinet and the governor's staff. Attending were Betty and Dr. Sam Ingram, Anne

and Brooks Parker, Bunny and Buck Allison, Mary and Tom Benson, Roma and Millard Oakley, Yvonne and General Carl Wallace, Jayne Ann and Frank Woods, Jo and Eddie Shaw, and Ruby and Dr. Eugene Fowinkle.[4] Special guests that evening included Ambassador Francis M. Deng, ambassador to the United States from Sudan, and Dr. Mansour Khalid, minister of education and culture, Khartoum, Sudan.

The following Sunday afternoon, the Blantons held an open house for the people of Tennessee. Mrs. Blanton said, "We are inviting all Tennesseans to come and visit us. We think the residence looks just beautiful and is something people will enjoy seeing." The focal point of the Yuletide decor at the executive residence that year was an eighteen-foot Scotch pine Christmas tree which was set up in the front foyer between the columns.[5] The following Christmas, the nation's bicentennial year of 1976, the Christmas tree, a live spruce, was decorated with ornaments given by garden clubs and other women's organizations across the state.

During their four years in the

90   TENNESSEE GOVERNORS AT HOME

executive residence, Governor and Mrs. Blanton hosted visits from many famous guests. Among them were U.S. First Lady Rosalyn Carter; Vice President Walter Mondale; President Gaafar el Nimeiri of Sudan; Prime Minister Julius Nyerere of Tanzania; and almost the entire body of the United Nations, led by Secretary General Kurt Waldheim.

As President Nimeiri's visit coincided with Nashville's premier charity event—the 1976 Swan Ball—Governor and Mrs. Blanton took their Harvard-educated guest to the ball, where he sat at a table next to Jane Dudley, the event's honorary chairperson and wife of Ambassador Guilford Dudley Jr.[6] The presence of the African leader caused problems in that Secret Service men had to check out all the people, such as Charles Kates and his catering staff, who had access to the tent before the ball. At the ball, a security agent sat in a chair immediately behind Mrs. Edward G. Nelson, who was seated on the other side of President Nimeiri. The plainclothesman was so close to Mrs. Nelson that his knees were in her back for much of the evening. Many guests were aware

of the publicity given President Nimeiri that steamy night. Certainly everyone at the Dudleys' table remembers the turban he wore to the event, particularly since he took it off and let another guest try it on. President Nimeiri brought his entire staff to Nashville. Mrs. Blanton's impression was that he did so, not because they were all friends of his, but to insure that there would not be a political coup while he was out of his country. To be sure that no mishaps befell Nimeiri's staff while in Tennessee, Governor Blanton assigned a state trooper to each member.[7] The Africans brought with them a "suitcase full of money" to buy American merchandise unavailable in their country. President Nimeiri also left an extremely generous tip for the maid at the executive residence.[8]

Prime Minister Nyerere's trade-related visit to Nashville came a year or so later. Ed Nelson, then president of Commerce Union Bank, recalls attending a dinner for the African leader at the executive residence. He enjoyed sitting at a table with actress Cicely Tyson and country music star Charlie Pride.[9] Mrs.

Governor and Mrs. Blanton. From *FBI Codename TENNPAR,* **by Hank Hillin, 1985.**

Blanton recalled the fact that the prime minister received part of his education at Nashville's Meharry Medical School.

Mrs. Jimmy Carter visited Nashville in May 1977 on behalf of one of her humanitarian causes. One of the necessities for the first lady's visit was the installation of a private line in her bedroom. The Blantons offered to have a dinner party for Mrs. Carter but she insisted that they not go to that trouble. Instead, the Blantons hosted a quiet family

Governor Blanton on December 7, 1977, singing a proclamation commemorating the anniversary of the bombing of Pearl Harbor. The ceremony was held at the executive residence in the sun room. TPS

dinner for her at the residence.[10]

Secretary General Kurt Waldheim came with nearly all of the United Nations representatives on June 6, 1976. The bicentennial trip was the first time the world body ever ventured outside New York City.[11] Mr. Waldheim, his wife, and daughter were the guests of the Blantons, who took them to one of the famous walking horse farms near Shelbyville where the Waldheims enjoyed riding the Tennessee walkers. On one

evening of the visit, the group went to the executive residence for dinner. The guests dined at round linen-covered tables set up on the terrace under a large tent. For entertainment, Charlie Pride, Dottie West, and the Oak Ridge Boys performed.

The Blantons also continued the practice, established by Betty Dunn, of opening the executive residence for two hours each Tuesday and Thursday afternoon for public visitation. Industrial recruitment also called for fre-

quent entertainment at the executive residence. On one occasion, when Nissan officials from Japan were there for dinner, Brenda Lee performed. This seemed natural because she had many Japanese fans, having traveled there a number of times. Besides, the diminutive Brenda said, she and the Japanese were the same size.[12]

One uninvited guest was Mrs. Jesse E. Wills of Nashville. One day, on a whim, she drove two friends from Little Rock, Arkansas, Gertrude Butler and Carrie Dickinson, to see the home where her mother-in-law, Jessie Ely Wills, formerly lived. Surprised to find a locked front gate, she blew her automobile's horn and, to the amazement of her guests, but not to her, the gates opened. Mrs. Wills then proceeded up the driveway to the circle at the entrance to the mansion. A state trooper politely asked if he could help. She said, "No thanks; I'm just showing my friends where Mrs. Wills used to live." He then asked her to wait a minute so Mrs. Blanton could speak to her. By this time, the guests were sliding down in their seats. In a moment or two, Mrs. Blanton, with her son David at her side, stepped outside and cordially spoke to the author's mother. Mrs. Wills's introductions were something less than impeccable since she could not remember Mrs. Blanton's first name. Gertrude Butler and Carrie Dickinson still enjoy laughing about that episode.[13]

The executive residence that guests and visitors saw during the Blanton administration was very much the same as that which people saw during the Dunn administration. Mrs. Blanton did not redecorate the executive residence in any meaningful way as state funds for such were scarce. She did remodel the kitchen and wanted to put needlepoint chairs in the formal dining room but was discouraged from doing so by Roupen Gulbenk, chairman of the Tennessee Executive Residence Preservation Foundation. She deferred to his judgement on the matter. Mrs. Blanton replaced Mrs. Dunn on the Tennessee Executive Residence Preservation Foundation and worked with the group to acquire additional items for the house. During the Blanton years, the foundation was instrumental in finding a Jonathan Gostelow Chippendale chest-on-chest with fine acanthus leaf carvings that was donated to the

Adjutant General Carl Wallace was appointed by Governor Blanton in 1975 to direct the state's military department. From *FBI Codename TENNPAR*, by Hank Hillin, 1985.

executive residence by Mrs. Hugh Stallworth and Mr. and Mrs. William I. Henderson, all of Nashville. Mrs. Blanton put the chest-on-chest in the drawing room.

A keen interest of Mrs. Blanton, while she served as the state's first lady, was in beautifying the executive residence

grounds.[14] During the Blanton administration, the Horn-of-Plenty Garden Club of Nashville took on the project of rebuilding the Wills's rock garden to the left of the driveway near the garage. Club members planted wild strawberries, wild roses, irises, and Dutchmen's Britches. Mrs. Blanton's flower gardens were

Governor and Mrs. Blanton entertaining visiting foreign dignitaries at the executive residence. TSLA

sufficiently prolific that in 1977 she told a reporter that, "We rarely ever buy cut flowers for the house—most of them come from the grounds."[15] A year earlier, the Tennessee Valley Authority gave a Ben Franklin flowering tree *(Franklinia altamaha)* to the executive residence on the nation's bicentennial. One of the nation's rarest trees, it was planted in the front lawn. In attendance were Dr. James Kelly, director of the Tennessee Bicentennial Commission; H. Peter Claussen, a TVA official; William L. Barry, chairman of the Tennessee Revolution Bicentennial Commission; and Mrs. Blanton.[16] Governor and Mrs. Blanton put a fountain in the middle of the reflecting pool where water lilies, many of which had been given by Sam Caldwell of Nashville, were growing. The fountain had been made for the Tennessee Park Service.[17] Inside the mansion, a fine Philadelphia chestnut chest, given by the Sack Foundation of Philadelphia and several Tennesseans, enhanced the drawing room. The Chippendale chest was built between 1760 and 1780.[18]

A good deal of Betty Blanton's energy during her years in the executive residence went into rearing her youngest son, Paul, then a student at nearby Franklin Road Academy. Paul especially loved a three-wheeler his parents bought him. One of his imagined duties was to be stationed at the electrically operated front gate when visitors were expected so that he could escort them up the driveway on his three-wheeler. Once, when he overturned, his cries were sufficiently loud for Hennie Benedict, who lived across the street, to hear them and come running to offer help. Fortunately, he was only scratched—not hurt. Paul's brother, David, being thirteen years older and out of school, enjoyed the privacy of an apartment in the garage, at least part of the time. Both boys enjoyed the family dog, Saki. They also had a Tennessee walking horse that someone gave Governor Blanton. While at the executive

residence, Saki had a litter of pups and the mare had a foal. The Blantons' daughter, Debbie Blanton Flack, was a frequent visitor. Her most memorable night was when she went into labor during a special dinner party for their young houseguests from Venezuela who were visiting Nashville during a Friendship Force Exchange.[19] Realizing that her labor promised to be long, Debbie did not go to the hospital until about 7:30 the next morning. That night, she and her husband, Lewis, got little sleep. She whiled away some of the nighttime hours drinking hot chocolate with the state troopers on duty downstairs. At the same time the Venezuelans were in Nashville, a group of Nashvillians, including David Blanton, were in Caracas staying with families there. When his mother asked how he got along on the

trip, David said that she should never get him involved in anything like that again. As the son of the governor of Tennessee, David was apparently looked upon to assume responsibilities in Venezuela he felt no reason to shoulder.

Governor and Mrs. Blanton ran into difficulties with their guests in that the Venezuelans thought that Mrs. Jimmy Carter would be in Nashville to greet them. They were upset upon learning that this was not the case. Mrs. Blanton went with a small group of them to Washington, D.C., where a visit with the first lady had been hastily arranged. This was a characteristically generous move by the forty-fifth first lady of Tennessee.

After leaving office in January 1979, Governor Blanton never served again in public office. He died on November 22, 1996.

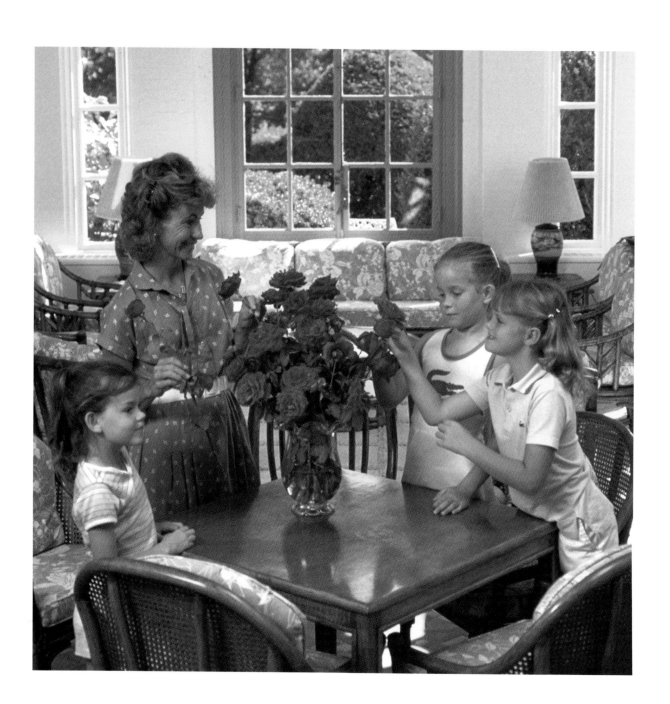

CHAPTER EIGHT

AN ACTIVE FAMILY SETTLES IN

Rᴇᴘᴜʙʟɪᴄᴀɴ Lᴀᴍᴀʀ Aʟᴇxᴀɴᴅᴇʀ ᴡᴀs ᴇʟᴇᴄᴛᴇᴅ ɢᴏᴠᴇʀɴᴏʀ ᴏꜰ Tennessee on November 7, 1978. On the following January 17, three days before he was to be sworn in as Tennessee's third Republican governor of the twentieth century, his schedule called for him to help his wife, Honey, five-months pregnant, move their family into the executive residence. That day, reports were circulating that outgoing governor Ray Blanton was selling prison pardons for cash. Alexander was advised by Hal Hardin, the United States attorney and a respected Democrat, to be sworn in early to stop any more prisoners from being released. Although initially stunned by this recommendation, Alexander accepted it after consultation with others, including House Speaker Ned Ray McWherter and Lieutenant Governor John Wilder. He and his staff began making the necessary arrangements. Having spent the day coordinating the move into the executive residence, when Mrs. Alexander was told by her husband what was about to happen, she said: "None of us have anything to

Governor and Mrs. Alexander walk with President Ronald Reagan and First Lady Nancy Reagan who visited the executive residence overnight in May, 1980. TPS

97

The Alexander family. Standing (left to right): Lamar, Honey, and Drew. Seated (left to right): Kathryn, Will, and Leslee. TSLA

wear to an inauguration this afternoon. The clothes are all in boxes at the governor's residence." Nevertheless, at 5:56 P.M., in a hurriedly arranged ceremony at the Tennessee Supreme Court, Lamar Alexander was sworn in as Tennessee's governor, and became the sixth governor to occupy the executive residence on South Curtiswood Lane.[1]

The Alexanders arrived at their new home "with three small children, dogs, guinea pigs, bikes, toys, and, most important, hopes to make this a real home."[2] For the next few days, they investigated their imposing new residence. While the executive residence looked beautiful on the outside, the interior was a different matter. The public areas badly needed refurbishing. "Draperies were threadbare and faded, rugs were worn and some of the rooms weren't exactly right," Honey Alexander recalled. The Alexanders also discovered an attic stuffed with furniture, and closets filled with boxes of items not being used. The accumulation of unneeded items went, as Mrs. Alexander said, "against my Scottish grain."

Almost immediately, she decided to get a decorator to help with redecorating. She thought of Tish Hooker, the ex-wife of John Jay Hooker, twice an unsuccessful Democratic candidate for governor. Tish, a decorator with Jay Thurman Interiors, was surprised to get Mrs. Alexander's call. "I thought she had the wrong number," Tish laughingly recalled. Mrs. Alexander told Tish, whom she knew only slightly, "I don't know anyone who's taken more of an interest in this house than you. I want you to do it."[3] Pleased to be asked to help decorate a home she had twice hoped to live in herself, Tish accepted.[4] "After all," she mused, "I wanted to be first lady even more than John Jay wanted to be governor."[5] Although the two women met and discussed their redecorating ideas, a year would pass before they could put their plans into action. In due time, the state legislature appropriated $100,000 for refurbishing the executive residence. With house money and the state appropriation, Mrs. Alexander hoped to start the project in the spring of 1980 and complete it by the following fall.

Even before they moved to the executive residence, the Alexanders had dinner with their good friends, former Governor Winfield Dunn and his wife, Betty. The Alexanders wanted to get the Dunns' input on the executive residence and how it might best be run. One piece of advice they received from the Dunns was to discontinue the system of employing prisoners as cooks, custodians, and grounds crew at the executive residence and to replace them with a professional staff.[6] Governor and Mrs. Alexander welcomed the suggestion. On the day before his family moved into the executive residence, Governor Alexander ordered that all the prisoners be returned to the main state prison.[7]

During the previous administration, one or more state troopers had always been on duty at a console and switchboard in the foyer. There, they could monitor activity at the front gate and elsewhere. The Alexanders moved the troopers' desk to the lower level. The reasoning for this change, as well as the decision regarding state prisoners, was that the Alexanders wanted their children to grow up in as normal an environment as possible. Two nights later, the Alexanders' daughter, six-year-old Leslee (Honey's "real" name)—an effervescent and assertive little character—telephoned from her second floor bedroom to the troopers' desk. She asked, "Will one of you-all bring me up a hamburger, a coke, and some french fries—large, please—to my room?" Fortunately, the trooper checked with Mrs. Alexander, who immediately went to Leslee's room and impressed on her daughter the importance of doing things for herself.[8]

In their first summer in the residence, the Alexanders enjoyed a new swimming pool and pool house, complete with

Governor Lamar Alexander. TSLA

kitchen, which were completed in July. The pool and pool house cost $38,000. This expense was not paid for by taxpayers but from funds left over from Governor Alexander's inauguration. The decking was made of stone from Crab Orchard, Tennessee, while the pool house columns were designed to match the executive residence's decor. The pool would become the scene of many summer parties for the children. In 1985, Leslee

ABOVE: Will Alexander by pool June, 1981. TPS

TOP: Drew Alexander celebrated his graduation with a party on May 31, 1984. TPS

hosted an end-of-year swimming party for her class at Ensworth School. The highlight of the party was a watermelon race the length of the pool. To make pushing the watermelons more difficult, the children greased them with Crisco. This left so much residue in the pool that it had to be thoroughly cleaned.[9]

Governor and Mrs. Alexander enjoyed playing tennis on the executive residence's tennis court with close friends. On Mother's Day 1979, when she was almost nine months pregnant, Mrs. Alexander and her partner, Dr. John S. Sergent, defeated the governor and his partner, Carole, Dr. Sergent's wife. The Alexander's fourth child, William Houston "Will" Alexander, was born the next day. He was the first child born to a Tennessee governor's wife during her husband's term of office in sixty-eight years.[10] As the tennis match suggests, Honey Alexander kept in excellent shape through daily exercise, including running in the neighborhood accompanied by her security person, trooper Hugh Hayes. Her neighbor, Andrew Benedict Jr., observed that she was a better runner than the security man. Undoubtedly, Mr. Benedict was

correct as, later, when Mrs. Alexander increased her distance to between three and one-half and four and one-half miles, Sergeant Hayes followed her in an automobile. As Mrs. Alexander said, "He's much happier now. Running is not his bag."[11]

Although caring for her four young children was her first priority, Mrs. Alexander was a gracious hostess and active first lady of Tennessee. She realized that it was important for her to be hostess for innumerable state dinners and other business affairs at the executive residence. For example, in September 1979, Honey hosted the families of Japanese businessmen who had moved to Tennessee. The children enjoyed swimming in the new pool and picnicking with their parents on the executive residence grounds.[12] The next month, the Friends of the Children's Hospital held a membership coffee at the executive residence.[13] At more formal dinners, Mrs. Alexander usually arranged to have honored Tennessee entertainers such as Chet Atkins perform. Such events went on continually.

Early in his administration, Governor Alexander hired

Anthony Colorio, formerly the executive chef at Nashville's Hyatt Regency Hotel, as chef at the executive residence.[14] Colorio's salary was $24,732 annually.[15] Until he arrived, breakfasts and lunches for the Alexander family and for security personnel were cooked by Ida Finch, a cook on loan from the state cafeteria. She recalled in 1998 that Governor Alexander loved peanut butter sandwiches with lettuce, mayonnaise, onions, and tomato. He often had that for lunch, she said, along with a bowl of tomato soup. According to Mrs. Finch, Mrs. Alexander preferred Mexican food and watercress sandwiches.[16] Ida, incidentally, was still working at the executive residence in 1999. Fred Love, another cook, came in each day at 11:00 A.M. to help with lunch and dinner. Besides Colorio, Governor Alexander's staff included an administrative assistant, Carole Martin; two custodians; one gardener; two food service supervisors; and three yard helpers, all employed by the Department of Public Works.[17] Jeanne Pearcy, whom the Alexanders had known from Westminster Presbyterian Church where she worked on the nursery

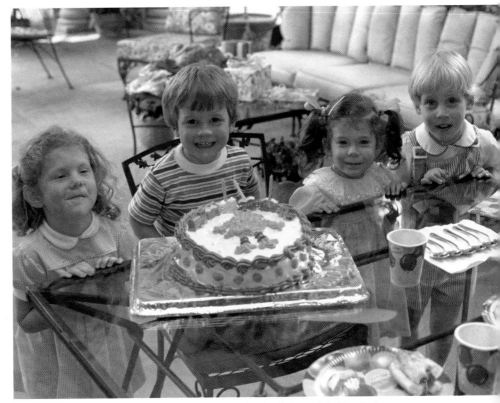

Will Alexander (second from left) celebrates his birthday with friends in May, 1983. TPS

staff, was employed to look after the children. She lived in the garage apartment at the executive residence.[18]

Christmas 1979 was much more relaxed than the previous one. In the two weeks before Christmas, the Alexanders hosted at the executive residence "the Capitol Hill press, Lamar's staff and cabinet, the Republican women, the residence's docents, and lots of friends" for receptions. Mrs. Alexander used fresh

fruit and greens as part of her Christmas decorations. Other decorations were in the Williamsburg style. Three Christmas trees were decorated each year. The Alexanders drove to Crossville to cut the trees at the University of Tennessee Experimental Station. The family tree in the drawing room was decorated by the family and featured the Alexanders' own ornaments, including many made by their children. The state tree stood in

David Keith (left), Minnie Pearl (center), and Patricia Neal (right) join Governor Alexander and staff at an event hosted for the Tennessee Film Commission. TPS

the foyer and was decorated by various civic organizations across the state. The third tree was the crafts tree, which stood in the sun room. It was decorated with ornaments donated by Tennessee craftsmen. On Christmas Eve the Alexanders worshiped at their church, Westminister Presbyterian. On Christmas Day, they opened their presents, enjoyed having the governor's parents relax with them, as the senior

Alexanders customarily did on Christmas, and had a roast beef dinner which Mrs. Alexander prepared herself. Her practice was to allow the staff to be at their own homes for Thanksgiving, Christmas, and alternate weekends when there was no official entertaining.[19]

On March 29, 1980, Mrs. Alexander hosted the first of many Easter egg hunts at the governor's residence. This one was

for mentally retarded children in Davidson County. Prizes were given for finding the silver and gold eggs and for finding the most eggs. Each child received an Easter basket. On such occasions, the Alexander children were on hand and often hid the eggs. They knew, however, not to participate.[20] When visitors were not around, the Alexander youngsters were less restrained. Occasionally, Will rode his tricycle and big wheeler on the mansion's hardwood floors and marble foyer, something the W. R. Wills grandchildren had done in the 1940s.

In March, the face-lifting project, which was to include new carpets, draperies, reupholstering, and wallpapering, was estimated to cost $89,000 and was to be completed by mid-August.[21] Once the renovation was completed, the executive residence became a secondary exhibition space for the Tennessee State Museum. Avron Fogelman, a prominent Memphis businessman and a new member of the Tennessee Executive Residence Preservation Foundation, pitched in by giving the mansion a "gorgeous new Steinway piano."[22] When he first saw the executive residence, it was obvious to him that "a lot of improvements were needed." The foundation sought out other Tennesseans who might be interested in helping with the restoration of the mansion. Among those who did were the grandchildren of Mr. and Mrs. W. R. Wills, the home's original owners. They gave a five-piece Sheffield tea service, circa 1810, in memory of their grandparents. The service was still on display in the dining room in 1999. After the renovation was completed, Fogleman reflected that, "We spent a lot of time and raised money privately and I can say there isn't much more to do. The mansion has the right look and feel of Tennessee."[23]

Later in the year, a replica of a solid mahogany candle stand table that General Andrew Jackson sat by when he opened his mail at The Hermitage was presented to the executive residence by Fred Tarkington Jr., owner of Tarkington Showroom of Nashville, and Mrs. Allen M. Steele, past regent of The Hermitage. The candle stand table given to the executive residence was the first of two hundred made by Davis Cabinet Company for the Century III Committee

 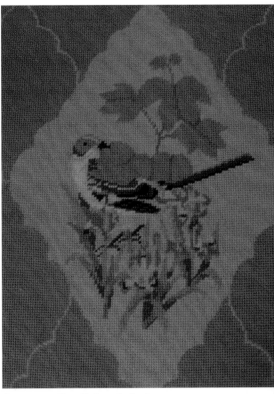

One of the needlepoint chair covers made for twenty-five dining chairs by a group from Memphis and Mrs. Alexander. The covers depict various blooming shrubbery, trees, flowers, and birds native to Tennessee. TPS

Project. The other candle stands were sold to the public to benefit The Hermitage.[24]

By spring 1980, Mrs. Alexander was also ready to deal with all the surplus furniture which had accumulated over eight gubernatorial terms. Decisions were made as to which furniture to keep. The surplus furnishings which could be used at other state properties were shipped out, and the Tennessee

State Museum was invited to take any items of historical significance. Finally, everything left over was offered for sale at a garage sale held at the Tennessee State Fairgrounds on June 21, 1980. As Mrs. Alexander stood on the sidelines watching, hundreds of Tennesseans bid on more than three hundred items. Among the items sold were a large reproduction Chippendale breakfront with fruitwood finish

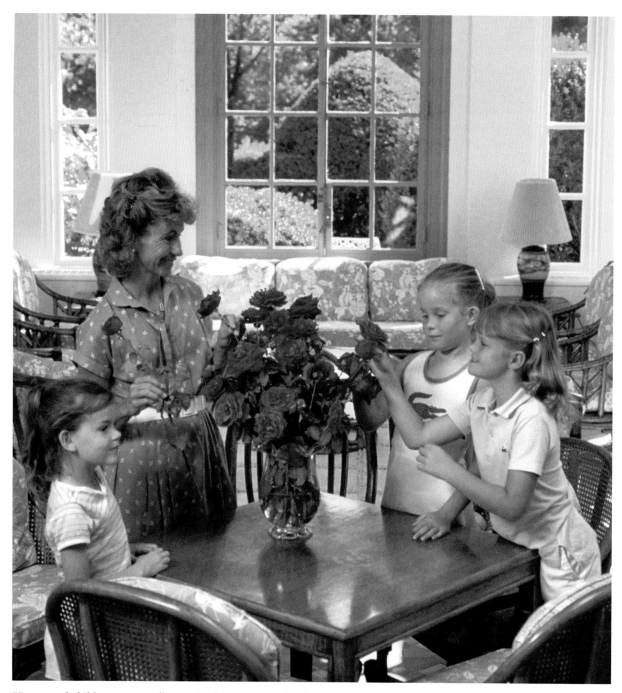

Honey and children arrange flowers in the sun room, 1981. TPS

TENNESSEE GOVERNORS AT HOME

and two valuable matching mirrors, eight feet tall, which had been bought by Governor and Mrs. Ellington. Also sold were other furniture, ovenware, vegetable bowls, coasters, Chinese figurines, bedspreads, books, and vases. It was hoped that the general state fund would benefit by $25,000 to $35,000 and it did.[25]

With the garage sale over, the Alexander family took an August vacation. Upon their return, they found twenty-four chairs with exquisite needlepoint seats that had been worked by twenty-four Memphis volunteers, including three men. The idea was conceived by Mrs. Perry Cockerham, a Memphis needlework shop owner, who had heard that Mrs. Alexander was considering a needlework project for the executive residence. She wrote the first lady and volunteered her services and those of other Memphians skilled in needlepoint work. The result was that the executive residence had fifteen small side chairs each uniquely covered with needlepoint in the design of Tennessee wildflowers. Each of ten large chairs had an individual design of blooming shrubbery and trees and birds native to Tennessee.[26] The delighted Mrs.

Alexander volunteered to do the needlepoint for the twenty-fifth chair.[27]

With new furniture and a refurbished downstairs, the Alexanders wanted to share the executive residence with the people of Tennessee who owned it. Just as the Blantons had done, they opened the mansion for free tours but with different hours and some new guides. The executive residence was open to the public each Tuesday and Thursday morning from 9:00 until 11:00 A.M. since this was when the Alexander children were in school.

For the Christmas holiday season, Mrs. Alexander added background music. Christmas visitors saw, upon entering the entrance foyer, a nine-and one-half-foot-tall blue spruce tree decorated with handmade ornaments designed by members of the Tennessee Embroidery Guild. School groups from various Metro Davidson County schools gave musical programs during the tours.[28]

Visitors to the executive residence could then see mementos that were meaningful to Governor Alexander. For example, in the governor's study on the

mantel, beneath a portrait of Sam Houston that had been given to the State of Tennessee from Texas friends, was a delightful collection of elephants, some wooden, some ivory, and others ceramic.[29] With them were several miniature donkeys that Mrs. Alexander had put in the governor's Christmas stocking "to keep him honest."[30] By the fireplace was Governor Alexander's collection of Tennessee walking sticks, including an iron one made by blacksmiths in Silver Dollar City at Pigeon Forge.[31] In the drawing room near the piano given by Avron Fogelman was a seventy-year-old grand piano that the governor owned. The Alexanders also had an upright piano in the third-floor playroom. Drew, Leslee, and Kathryn all took piano lessons, following in the footsteps of their father, who has long enjoyed playing the piano.[32]

Before the renovation, the sunroom had heavy red velvet drapes, which kept out the sunlight, and a rather worn carpet. As the room was not bright, the first lady wondered why it was called the sunroom. To make the name more fitting, she removed the drapes, allowing the sunshine to pour in, and got rid of the rug, exposing the beautiful tile floor which was original to the house.[33] Mrs. Alexander also brought in lightly colored summer cane furniture and displayed the art work of Tennessee artists and craftsmen, including some rotating exhibits from the Tennessee State Museum.[34]

The family dining room was named the Greeneville Room during the Alexander years. Greene County Tennesseans, under the leadership of *Greeneville Sun* publisher John M. Jones, donated the antiques, all made in Greene County, for the room. The furniture included a country Sheraton, two-part cherry banquet table, circa 1815; a cherry broken-arch corner cupboard, circa 1800; a cherry solid-end chest, also built circa 1800; and a set of six Windsor chairs reproduced by Claude Phillips, a Greeneville craftsman. A copy of the portrait of Andrew Johnson by Samuel Shaver that now hangs in the parlor of the Andrew Johnson home in Greeneville was also included.[35]

On another wall, Mrs. Alexander hung a painting called *Mountains* by Carl Sublett, a University of Tennessee professor

of art. The painting was a cherished birthday gift from her husband, in part because it reminded Honey of the view the Alexanders saw from the front porch of their cabin in Blount County.[36]

Although Leslee and Kathryn's bedrooms were not normally seen by visitors, they featured twin four-poster beds covered in a blue and white etoile print.[37]

Drew's room included the usual things an eleven-year-old boy could be expected to have, including caged pet mice and an electric train. The children also had plastic big wheelers; several dogs, including two cocker spaniels, Lady and Corfe; a rabbit that lived in a cage beside a tree outside the kitchen window; and a golf cart that arrived in 1986.

When Mrs. Alexander's friends drove up the driveway, they were likely to encounter Will and a friend, John Austin Echols, flying down the hill in their big wheelers.[38] The boys would peel off into the ditches at the last moment, giving the visitors visions of having injured one of the governor's children. Lady usually stuck close to Will while Corfe could often be found on the

floor beside Mrs. Alexander's desk in her small office upstairs. One day Lady snatched Will's white blanket and tore out the front door to bury it in the yard. Upset at the loss of one of his treasured possessions, Will began to holler. The state trooper stationed downstairs retrieved the blanket and all was soon well.[39]

Throughout the Alexander years, a number of famous people were overnight guests at the executive residence. Among them were Senator Howard Baker; President and Mrs. Gerald Ford; President and Mrs. Ronald Reagan, who spent the night in May 1980; then-Vice President and Mrs. George Bush; and actress Elizabeth Taylor.[40] Of all the national figures who were overnight guests, Elizabeth Taylor caused the most excitement among the staff. Alex Haley, the celebrated author of *Roots* and a good friend of the Alexander family, ran a close second. Following these visits, the Alexanders called the guest bedroom where the Reagans, the Gerald Fords, the George Bushes, and Elizabeth Taylor stayed during their respective visits the Elizabeth Taylor Room.[41]

On their last night in the executive residence, the governor and first lady retired early to watch *On the Beach* on television. Their daughter Kathryn peeked in the packed-up bedroom and said, "You-all's room looks so sad and empty."[42] The next day, Governor Alexander recalled that "the big house was quiet and empty." Seeing the packed boxes on the floor made him reflect on the growth and changes in the state that he had seen in the past eight years. He also thought about the changes in his own family and the fact that his young son, Will, then seven and one-half, had not even been born when he was sworn in as governor. He said that Will "moved today out of the only home he has ever known."[43]

Following his eight years as governor, Lamar Alexander and his family took a six-month vacation to Australia. As Mrs. Alexander said before the trip, "We've got to get out of here—a long way away and for a long time, maybe six months. We need

Like her father, Kathryn enjoys playing the piano. TPS

to be a family again and you need some time to think about what to do with the rest of your life."

Following their return, Governor Alexander finished writing his third book, *Six Months Off: An American Family's Australian Adventure*. He then went on to become president of the University of Tennessee, secretary of education under President Bush, and a presidential contender in the 1996 and the 2000 Republican primaries.

CHAPTER NINE

THE FIRST
BACHELOR SINCE
PRENTICE COOPER

Governor McWherter
and family (left to right):
Brett Ramsey, Steve
Ramsey, Matthew
Ramsey, Linda Ramsey,
Governor McWherter
holding his grandson,
Walker Ray McWherter,
and Michael Ray
McWherter. Seated:
Mary Jane McWherter
holding Mary Bess
McWherter. NRM

NED RAY MCWHERTER WAS THE SEVENTH GOVERNOR TO reside in the residence on South Curtiswood Lane. A few days before his inauguration, he received a letter from Walter G. Knestrick, a prominent Nashville businessman and art collector. Knestrick had, during Governor Alexander's administration, given the State of Tennessee an oil painting of General Andrew Jackson at the Battle of New Orleans. Governor Alexander, a friend of Knestrick's, had hung it in the executive residence. Knestrick wrote the new governor a note telling him that he should not feel obligated to keep the painting by Edward Moran and that, if he did not want it, he should call Lois Riggins-Ezzell, executive director of the Tennessee State Museum, who was prepared to have it removed.

McWherter immediately called and said he "loved Andrew Jackson" and would like to keep the painting at the residence. When McWherter made the telephone call to Knestrick, he introduced himself quite informally, saying "This is Ned Ray." Knestrick, as an

Governor Ned Ray McWherter. TSLA

avid Alexander supporter and a Republican fund-raiser, had not anticipated getting a call from the governor-elect and thought he was talking to one of the supervisors at his construction company. When it dawned on him exactly who was speaking, beads of sweat popped out on his brow, and Knestrick said, as only he would, "Oh yes, your excellency, you may keep the painting as long as you are in office."[1]

Ned McWherter did not get to enjoy the Jackson painting immediately. Although the Alexanders had moved out three days before his inauguration, the new governor realized that the upstairs of the mansion was badly antiquated in terms of its plumbing and wiring, and that some of the bedroom and bathroom walls needed repainting. He wanted to get those matters taken care of before moving in. While the second floor was being remodeled, Governor McWherter continued to live in his condominium in Nashville. His mother, Lucille McWherter, lived in the executive residence's guest bedroom during this period. To keep her company, Ned's unmarried son, Michael Ray "Mike" McWherter, then a Nashville attorney, moved into the executive residence for about six months.[2]

Mrs. McWherter, whom the governor referred to as his "first lady," doted on her son and sometimes fixed him his favorite breakfast of country-style bacon with the rind left on and scrambled eggs cooked with macaroni and cheese. For lunch, Governor McWherter enjoyed eating a fried bologna sandwich. He has also

always been partial to hot-water cornbread.[3]

Lucille McWherter died of cancer in April 1987. It was during his mother's final illness that Governor McWherter's next door neighbor, Sarah Cannon, who had a history of cancer herself, was a compassionate and thoughtful friend. A few months after Mrs. McWherter's death, Mrs. Cannon, best known as Minnie Pearl, eulogized the governor's mother with these words: "She was a model of Southern determination and grit, not only for her son, but for all Tennesseans." Minnie Pearl also recalled having asked Mrs. McWherter if she raised her son to be governor. According to Minnie, Mrs. McWherter said, "I raised him to be president. I wonder what's taking so long."[4]

Governor Ned McWherter's remodeled living quarters were in the west wing. They included a master bedroom with bath, a sitting room, and a study-library. At some point, Governor McWherter added a Jacuzzi in the master bathroom. In the east wing were three guest bedrooms with baths, an office for the governor's personal assistant, Mrs. Madelyn Pritchett, and a small utility room/kitchen. A group of Tennesseans including Mr. Ray Bell, Mr. and Mrs. Dennis Bortorff, Mr. and Mrs. John Clay Jr., Mr. and Mrs. Tom Cone, Mr. and Mrs. David D. Dortch, Mr. and Mrs. John Hailey, Mr. and Mrs. Larry Lipman, Mr. and Mrs. Hank McCall, and Mr. and Mrs. Fred Viehmann made the renovations possible.[5] The third floor was used as a large playroom for Governor McWherter's four grandchildren, Brett and Matt Ramsey, and Walker Ray and Mary Bess McWherter.[6] In his study, the governor added his personal touch by keeping a jar full of vanilla wafers on his desk. They were a reminder of his campaign pledge: "I'll be a first-day governor. Give me a cup of coffee, four vanilla wafers, and I'll be ready to go to work."

During the McWherter years, the ten-acre executive residence grounds included the garage, greenhouse, seasonal flower beds, native hardwood trees, fruit trees, the swimming pool and pool house built during the Alexander years, tennis court, and a memorial garden of Minnie Pearl roses that Governor McWherter built to honor his mother, Lucille Smith McWherter.

Billy and Alma Ford were employed by the governor to live in an existing garage apartment as caretakers for the property. There was also a small fort in the yard, built for the Alexander children, that McWherter's grandchildren enjoyed. The two oldest, Brett and Matt Ramsey, loved to roam around the grounds on a golf cart Governor McWherter inherited from the Alexanders. Inside, the breakfast room, still called the Greeneville Room, showed considerable wear and tear on the antique furniture. Governor McWherter, a big man, had the skirt sawed off the antique table so he could get his legs beneath it. As he was afraid to sit in the small Windsor chairs, he moved a comfortable chair into the room and moved the six Windsor chairs out.

Just as Governor and Mrs. Alexander had done, Governor McWherter opened the executive residence to the public for tours each Tuesday and Thursday from 1:00 until 3:00 in the afternoon. The tours which were free, could be arranged by calling the executive residence in advance.

Tourists in buses and automobiles frequently rode slowly on South Curtiswood Lane to take photographs of the

Vice President Gore visiting with Governor McWherter. TPS

Tennessee executive residence. Although they were not supposed to stop, some did. One day when a tour bus stopped near the front entrance and people got out for a better look, Henry Cannon happened to be planting a bush in his front yard nearby. One lady walked over and asked Henry, who was wearing overalls, "Do you work here?" He said that he did. She then asked how long he had

ABOVE: Governor McWherter at the Lucille McWherter Rose Garden amid Minnie Pearl roses. The garden was established by the Nashville Rose Society in memory of the governor's mother. NRM

RIGHT: Governor McWherter at his desk in the executive residence. TPS

worked there. Henry dead-panned, "As long as Minnie Pearl has lived here." Still interested, the lady next asked if he was well paid. Mr. Cannon replied, "No, but, if I do a good job, she lets me sleep with her." The lady got back on the bus without asking any more questions.[7]

Sarah and Henry Cannon were close friends of Governor McWherter. Often, they had dinner together. After Sarah Cannon suffered a stroke, the governor would sometimes drop by her house in the afternoons for a visit. On his arrival, Sarah was apt to ask Henry to fix them a "little toddy," usually of Maker's Mark bourbon. With a wink, Sarah would say that "Of course, we don't drink before 5:00 P.M., but it has to be 5:00 P.M. somewhere."[8] On those occasions, the governor enjoyed hearing the Cannons' stories about Hank Williams and the Grand Ole Opry.[9]

To celebrate the bicentennial of the signing of the United States Constitution, the museum made arrangements, two years in advance, for one of the four original copies of the Magna Carta (772 years old at the time) and an annotated copy of the United States Constitution to be displayed at the Tennessee State Museum.[10] The exhibit, which was entitled, "Magna Carta: Liberty under the Law," opened on September 17, 1987, the two-hundredth anniversary of the signing of the U.S. Constitution. Lord Hailsham, a former English

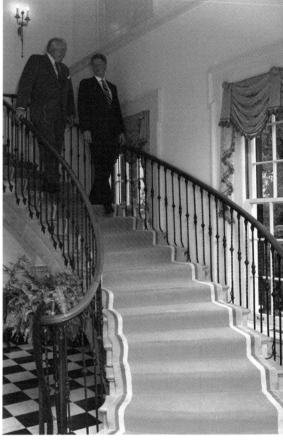

ABOVE: Governor McWherter giving a tour of the executive residence to his friend President William Jefferson Clinton. TPS

LEFT: Governor McWherter, First Lady Hillary Rodham Clinton, and President Clinton. TSLA

FOLLOWING PAGES: Governor McWherter poses for an informal tour of the executive residence with the state photographer. TPS

Parliament member and recently retired Lord Chancellor, flew to Nashville with Lady Hailsham for a number of public appearances related to the Magna Carta exhibit, including a reception in the Tennessee State Museum. The English statesman and orator, who would celebrate his eightieth birthday a few weeks later, was invited to participate in the ceremonies because his mother, the former Myssy Brown, was a Nashville native and the granddaughter of Neill S. Brown, Tennessee's governor from 1847 to 1849.[11] While in Nashville, Lord and Lady Hailsham stayed at the residence for a week as the guests of Governor McWherter. There, Lord Hailsham regaled the governor with stories of World War II.

The Magna Carta almost didn't make it to the exhibit. The Tennessee side of the story is that officials with the Federal Bicentennial Commission wanted to ship the document to Nashville the day *after* September 17 so it would still be on display in Philadelphia, Pennsylvania on the two-hundredth anniversary of the U.S. Constitution. To resolve the impasse, Governor McWherter sent Lois Riggins-Ezzell, executive director of the Tennessee State Museum, an assistant state attorney general, and a U.S. Marshal to New York on a state jet to get the Magna Carta. They did so successfully with the help of two lawyers retained in New York.[12]

The following month, Her Royal Highness Princess Ann of Great Britain came to Nashville

to participate in the first annual Royal Chase at Warner Park. The Princess Royal was the first member of the royal family to compete in a racing event in the United States. On the afternoon of the event, she also presented the winner's cup to the victor in the Queen Mother Supreme Novice Chase, named in honor of her grandmother. Governor McWherter, who was honorary chairman of the Nashville Committee for The Royal Chase, hosted a reception for Princess Ann and other English visitors who also had come to Nashville for the event. Before the reception, his Nashville friends Jane Dudley and Alyne Massey schooled him in the proper etiquette for greeting visiting royalty.[13] Other visitors to the Tennessee executive residence

TENNESSEE GOVERNORS AT HOME

during Governor McWherter's administration included President and Mrs. Clinton. President Clinton came both when he was governor of Arkansas and when he was running for president. Because Nashville then had an American Airlines hub, it was convenient for Governor Clinton, while campaigning, to stop over in Nashville for a few hours before returning to Little Rock. On one occasion, when Governor and Mrs. Clinton were at the executive residence, Governor McWherter's son, Mike, was also there with his wife, Mary Jane, and their baby, Walker. That evening, Mike was having difficulty getting Walker to burp. Mrs. Clinton, who was dressed for a formal party at the Opryland Hotel, took Walker on her shoulder and succeeded in

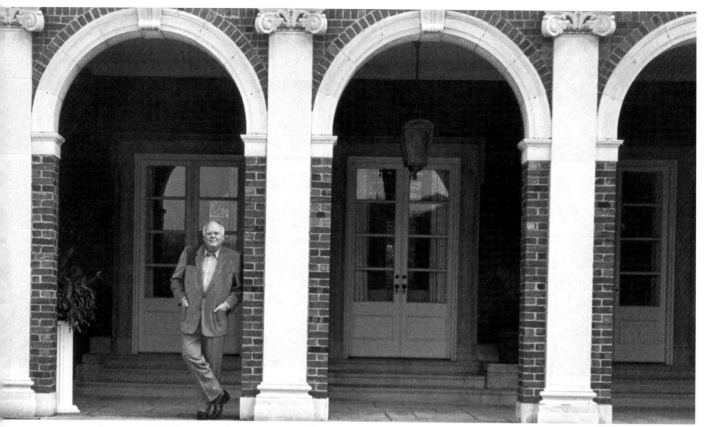

Governor McWherter at the executive residence. NRM

burping him. Unfortunately, Walker spit up on the back of her dress. Undaunted, she handled the situation gracefully. Mrs. Clinton told Mike and Mary Jane, "Don't worry. Nobody will notice. But if they do, every mother will know exactly what happened and will explain the situation to anyone who does not."[14] Either that time, or on another occasion, the Clintons came to Nashville for a Jackson Day Dinner at the Opryland Hotel. The speaker for the event was Jay Rockefeller, at that time the governor of West Virginia and a houseguest of Governor McWherter. During the dinner, Governor Rockefeller choked on a piece of steak that had lodged in his throat. He had to be taken to Vanderbilt Hospital to have it removed. Governor McWherter asked Governor Clinton to take Governor Rockefeller's place as the speaker that evening. Governor Clinton, seldom at a loss for words, was glad to do so even on such a short notice. Concerned that he might speak too long, Governor McWherter asked him "to keep it short"[15] (presumably, he did). Senators Lloyd Benson of Texas, Senator Charles Robb of Virginia, and the Chinese ambassador and his wife also visited the executive residence. Vice President Albert Gore

116

and his wife, Tipper, came on several occasions. Before the visit by Senator Benson, Secret Service agents wanted to flip over the mattress on the governor's bed while he was getting dressed in the room. McWherter said, "No deal."[16]

A tradition in the McWherter family was that the entire family got together each Thanksgiving and each Christmas. So, for each of the years he was governor, Ned McWherter hosted a festive family dinner on those holidays for his son, Mike; his daughter, Linda Ramsey; her husband, Steve; and their boys. After Mike married in 1989, his wife, Mary Jane and, in time, their children, Walker and Bess, were included. Mike McWherter gave up his Nashville law practice in 1990 and moved to Jackson, Tennessee, to enter the family business. After that, he and Mary Jane never dropped in at the executive residence unexpectedly because they knew that there was likely to be a group of businessmen there. Mike's feeling is that his father used the executive residence more for state business than perhaps any of his predecessors. As Governor McWherter was single, he continually enter-

tained executive officers of companies interested in relocating to Tennessee. Often, prominent Nashville country music stars provided the entertainment.[17]

Because of the tremendous pressures incumbent with being the governor of Tennessee, Ned McWherter would seek ways to relax and to temporarily put aside the myriad problems which he faced on Capitol Hill. He particularly would enjoy putting on a pair of boots, khaki pants, and work shirt and driving his jeep out to Radnor Lake State Natural Area to walk on the footpaths and enjoy the serenity of that beautiful site. This brief retreat reminded him of the Obion River bottoms of his native West Tennessee. Returning to the executive residence from Radnor Lake late one afternoon, McWherter announced his presence at the gated entrance. Because the sun had gone down and the officer on duty was new to the job, he did not recognize the governor's jeep. Consequently, he asked over the intercom, "Who is it?" The governor replied, "Ned." The guard then said, "Ned who?" Governor McWherter said, "Ned Ray McWherter." The gates were

Governor McWherter watching poolside activites at the executive residence. TPS

quickly opened by an embarrassed trooper.

Sometime during Governor McWherter's years as governor, his office got a call from someone at the Pentagon, asking that the Gorham punch bowl and silver cups that had been on the sideboard at the Tennessee executive residence since 1971 be returned to the United States government as the Navy planned to commission a submarine to be named the USS *Tennessee* and wanted to place the silver service in the submarine's officers' wardroom. Governor McWherter enlisted the assistance of Howard Baker, then

Governor McWherter enjoying Thanksgiving dinner with his family at the executive residence, 1993. NRM

chief of staff under President Reagan, to keep the punch bowl and cups permanently at the executive residence. With Senator Baker's help, the United States Navy agreed to accept a new silver punchbowl and cups, paid for by friends of the governor, and to leave the original pieces in the care of the Tennessee State Museum.[18]

Governor McWherter also narrowly missed losing two handsome chandeliers that hung in the executive residence's front entrance hall. One day he entered the residence only to find one of the chandeliers lying on the carpet in the entrance hall. Having determined that no one was hurt when the chandelier fell, he had all the other chandeliers in the house checked to be certain that they were secure. Despite this precaution, the second chandelier in the front hall fell about two weeks later. Because some prisms on both chandeliers were broken when they fell, the person who repaired the chandeliers was forced to put all the unbroken prisms on one chandelier. The other chandelier was still without prisms when Governor McWherter left office.[19]

One day in the fall of 1994, not long before Governor McWherter left office, he got a telephone call from Frank G. Clement Jr. who had supported Governor McWherter in his gubernatorial campaigns. Frank asked if he might bring his daughter, Jennifer, to the governor's residence to show her the house where he had spent so many pleasurable years when he was a boy. Governor McWherter who was known for being outgoing and gracious, arranged for Frank, his wife, Erma, and daughter Jennifer to have lunch with him at the executive residence on Jennifer's thirteenth birthday, October 1. Because Governor McWherter was going to be out of the house the remainder of the day, he cordially gave Frank permission to show Erma and Jennifer every nook and cranny of the house that afternoon. They did so, exploring rooms from basement to attic.[20]

Governor McWherter left the executive residence at 10:00 P.M. on his last day in office. One of his last-minute concerns was that some of the flooring in the master bedroom and bath was rotten, probably having to do with the

Jacuzzi in the latter room. He wanted to have the bad flooring replaced before the Sundquists took possession of the executive residence the next day. Governor McWherter called on his close friend, Peaches Simpkins,[21] to get the job done. Late in the afternoon of the governor's last day in office, Peaches was on the phone with a flooring contractor with whom she had done business in the past. She told him that Governor McWherter wanted the flooring taken up and replaced by eight the next morning. The man first said that was impossible.

Peaches retorted by saying, "I'll give you the governor's private telephone number. You call him and tell him it is impossible." After a little more persuasion, the contractor agreed to have his workmen come to the executive residence that evening and work through the night to complete the job. The next morning it was done.[22]

Since retiring from public office, Governor McWherter has devoted his time to his varied business interests. He lives in Dresden, Tennessee, has a farm in Weakley County, and a home on a bluff overlooking the Tennessee River at Buchanan, Tennessee. He is chairman of the board of Volunteer Distributing in Dresden; Central Distributors in Jackson, Tennessee; Volunteer Express, a Nashville-based trucking company; and Weakley County Bank in Dresden. He additionally serves on the boards of Coca-Cola Bottling Company, Consolidated; Piedmont Natural Gas Company; and SunTrust Bank, Nashville, N.A. He also is one of the nine members of the Board of Governors for the United States Postal Service.

CHAPTER TEN
MARTHA AND DON SUNDQUIST

ONCE THEY HAD MOVED INTO THE EXECUTIVE RESIDENCE AT 882 South Curtiswood Lane, Martha Sundquist, the wife of Don Sundquist, the twenty-eighth governor of Tennessee, demonstrated a keen interest in displaying the work of Tennessee artists and craftsmen there and acquiring books written by Tennessee authors for its library. It was natural then that the Tennessee Executive Residence Foundation, after being relatively inactive during the previous two administrations, met early in the Sundquist administration to identify a number of Tennesseans who might be interested in purchasing furniture or fine art for the executive residence.[1] As a result of the meeting, Governor and Mrs. Sundquist hosted a dinner at the mansion for a number of potential donors. Following that dinner, the foundation acquired a number of significant pieces, including a Philadelphia Chippendale mirror similar to one at Mount Vernon and a museum-quality blocked-front Chippendale chest from Massachusetts. The chest was made possible through gifts from Jim

Governor and Mrs. Sundquist admiring the reflecting pool on the grounds of the executive residence. TPS

121

Governor Don Sundquist. TSLA

cocks that had originally been at the residence when it was the home of Mr. Wills's grandparents, Mr. and Mrs. Ridley Wills. Mrs. Sundquist drove out to Meeting of the Waters, the Wills's home in Williamson County, to pick up the peacocks, thus insuring that they had a safe ride back to the executive residence, where they now flank the steps leading to the reflecting pool in the garden. An inlaid card table for the executive dining room was also given during this period by Nashville architect Earl S. Swensson and his wife, Sue. Friends from Memphis, under the leadership of Kathy (Mrs. Dwight) Clark, made possible the acquisition of a Tennessee sideboard, probably made in Nashville about 1815. The cherry sideboard, which stands in the hallway outside the governor's office, features a rectangular top with a plain front edge, turned legs, a convex center drawer, a beaded, arched center section, and glass knobs.

During the first year of the Sundquist administration, major renovations were made to the mansion. These included such necessities as updating the heating and air-conditioning system,

repairing the slate roof, and modernizing the security system.

The Sundquists had always been dog lovers and the house seemed to be missing something without a dog around. Mrs. Sundquist refused to discuss a puppy, knowing from years of experience that a puppy would require too much time for training as well as be apt to chew on things he wasn't supposed to. So they were very excited when they went to eat one evening at a neighborhood restaurant and the waitress, who was from England, said she was moving back home and was worried about the beautiful golden retriever she had been feeding and taking care of. His name was Bailey, named for Bailey's Irish Cream. The governor immediately loaded the dog into the car, thinking he had found the perfect solution to the void at the residence.

Things went well for a month or so until a Nashville television station decided to do a personal interest story on Governor Sundquist and his dog. Of special interest was the fact that the governor had to carry this large dog over the marble entry hall because Bailey found it too slippery to walk on. The day after the

and Natalie Haslam and Mr. and Mrs. Ross N. Faires, all of Knoxville, and the Hyde Family Foundation in Memphis. The mirror, which was hung over the chest in the mansion's entrance hall, was acquired through the generosity of Mr. and Mrs. William Looper of Columbia. Irene and Ridley Wills II, of Franklin, donated two lead pea-

ABOVE: Governor and Mrs. Sundquist greet well-wishers at the executive residence after the governor's inauguration, January 1995. TPS

LEFT: First Lady Martha Sundquist and Ruby on the front lawn for a photo to promote the Department of Agriculture's "Pick Tennessee Products" campaign in which Mrs. Sundquist served as spokesperson. TPS

Governor and Mrs. Sundquist and the Easter Bunny with kindergartners from McFadden Elementary School in Murfreesboro, Tennessee. TPS

year later and put to sleep after twenty days.

After this experience the Sundquists went to the Nashville Humane Association shelter and selected two dogs, Ruby, a black Labrador, and Millie, a brown mixed breed. The family pets have found a happy home exploring the ten acres at the residence and chasing squirrels and moles.[2]

Because the executive residence is owned by the people of Tennessee, Volunteer State governors and their spouses have long felt an obligation to open the house to the public when they could. The Sundquists have been gracious in this respect. At their first reception, held the first Sunday following Governor Sundquist's inauguration, he and Mrs. Sundquist shook hands in a receiving line for six hours. After recovering from that ordeal and when the renovation of the house was complete, Mrs. Sundquist felt more comfortable inviting the public to see it.

In addition to having docents show visitors through the executive residence two mornings each week, Mrs. Sundquist soon established two annual events as her own.

special aired, the governor received a call informing him that the dog belonged to some people who lived several blocks from the restaurant. After the Sundquists checked out the story to make sure it was true, Bailey was reunited with an eleven-year-old boy. What should have been a happy ending turned sad when the dog that loved to roam was picked up by the Metro Pound a

Each spring, she hosts an Easter egg roll for underprivileged children. The first time she hosted this event, the executive residence was nearly overrun with children. Since then, Mrs. Sundquist has found that about 125 children of kindergarten age is the maximum number she and her staff can conveniently handle. The children come with their teachers from various schools and community centers. Once at the executive residence, the children are divided into four groups. A magician entertains one group while Mother Goose holds forth in another. In a third area, a group takes part in face painting, while the final group has fun with an egg roll in which many eggs are broken but no child is a loser. Each child leaves with a bag filled with candy, a book, pencils, and a wooden Easter egg with the date and "Tennessee Executive Residence" stenciled on it.[3]

The other event Mrs. Sundquist feels ownership of is a Swedish holiday celebration to which she invites other Middle Tennesseans of Swedish descent. The party is in honor of Saint Lucia, the medieval saint who brings light to Swedish homes each December 13. On that day

LEFT: A Saint Lucia doll serving as a centerpiece for the annual Saint Lucia breakfast at the executive residence. TPS

RIGHT: Tania Sundquist Williamson as Saint Lucia, 1996. TPS

in towns all across Sweden, girls, preferably ones with long, blond hair, are chosen to play the role of Lucia. Traditionally they wear white, full-length chemises, with red ribbons around their waists and wreaths of lingonberry sprigs on their heads. The wreaths have

holders for real candles or battery-powered ones to give the effect of halos.[4] Each year, Mrs. Sundquist invites a young woman to play the role of Lucia; in 1996, the Sundquists' eldest daughter, Tania, played the part. The first lady's role in the celebration is to

LEFT TO RIGHT: Governors Dunn, McWherter, Sundquist, and Alexander gather on the day of neighbor Minnie Pearl's funeral. TSLA

bake Swedish coffee bread for the Saint Lucia breakfast. Mrs. Sundquist got the idea for the Lucia celebration when she and her husband, also of Swedish heritage, were students at Augustana College in Rock Island, Illinois. Augustana, one of the oldest of the colleges founded by Scandinavian Lutherans in America, still maintains the custom of having a Lucia celebration each December 13.[5]

In the first year of their administration, Governor and Mrs. Sundquist paid a visit to their next door neighbor, Sarah Cannon, who was then in a nursing home. At some point, Governor Sundquist, who enjoys humor, started to tell a joke. Mrs. Cannon, known to millions as "Cousin Minnie Pearl," raised her hand and said, "Stop, stop right there! I don't meddle in pol-

itics; you don't need to meddle in comedy." Mrs. Cannon's great sense of humor remained to the end. At an auction follwing her death, the Sundquists purchased a beautiful silver and cut-glass dish that Mrs. Cannon kept potpourri in, as well as a silver bud vase with her name engraved on it. Mrs. Sundquist keeps fresh flowers in the bud vase in Sarah Cannon's memory. Both pieces

TENNESSEE GOVERNORS AT HOME

are on display in the small sitting room at the executive residence.[6]

The Sundquists also annually open the executive residence for Halloween trick-or-treaters from the Franklin Road area. In 1998, they dressed up as members of the Addams family with the first lady playing the role of Morticia, the governor the role of Uncle Fester, and their daughter, Tania, as Wednesday. Two hundred children and their parents enjoyed the event.[7]

There are few nights that the Sundquists are home that they don't have visitors. About once a month, Governor Sundquist invites fifteen or twenty Tennesseans for a Sunday soiree. Country music stars Hank Williams Jr., Brenda Lee, Mark Collie, and George Jones have attended as have Tennessee's state poet Maggi Vaughn, Tennessee historian and author Wilma Dykeman, musician Michael W. Smith, and race car drivers Coo Coo and Sterling Marlin. The Sundquists use these occasions to honor deserving Tennesseans such as John Rice Irwin, the owner of the Museum of Appalachia in Norris, Tennessee; or John Netherton, the Nashville nature photographer whose work has

A Tennessee 200 Bicentennial event—First Ladies Day, December 1995, at The Hermitage, home of President Andrew Jackson. Seated (left to right): Martha Sundquist, Catherine Ellington, Hortense Cooper. Standing (left to right): Honey Alexander, Betty Blanton, Daisy King (Tennessee's First Lady of Southern Cooking), and Betty Dunn.

been featured in eight of his own books and in hundreds of magazines.[8] William R. Snodgrass, the comptroller of the treasury, who retired after over fifty years of service to the state, was honored at such a dinner in 1999.

The Sundquists host a party twice annually for the press and the governor's cabinet. The summer party, held on the grounds, typically features shrimp and oysters, hot dogs, hamburg-ers, and potato salad. Its feature event is an egg toss with the press pitted against the administration. After four straight losses to the press, the administration was able to pull off a victory in 1999. The other party for the press corps and the administration is held at Christmastime. The 1998 Capitol Hill press corps party was held December 14, just after Governor Sundquist returned from a successful ten-day business-recruiting

Mrs. Sundquist with Santa at the press holiday party. TPS

trip to Japan. Other holiday receptions are given for the governor's staff, for the members of the Tennessee General Assembly, for the people who work at the executive residence, and for the docents who give so freely of their time to give tours of the residence. At one executive residence reception, State Senator John Ford of Memphis parked his car on the gray cobblestone circle in front of the house. Someone reported that he parked on the governor's helicopter pad![9]

For Christmas 1997, The Sundquists hosted open houses on Sunday, December 7, for East and West Tennesseans and on the following Sunday for Middle Tennesseans interested in seeing the residence decorated for the holiday season. Mrs. Sundquist counted one thousand punch cups that were used during the two receptions. Governor and Mrs. Sundquist greeted the visitors and posed for photographs in front of a Christmas tree in the mansion's formal living room. Down the hall in the foyer, beside the winding staircase, was another Christmas tree, this one festooned with bears, tiny

carousels, dolls, and baby shoes. Two merry-go-round horses and a little lamb sat beside the tree. The decorations and toys were in honor of the Sundquists' then six-month old granddaughter, Gabrielle Renee Jeannet, who arrived from Phoenix, Arizona, with her parents, Andrea and Art Jeannet, a few days before Christmas.

On April 15, 1998, Governor and Mrs. Sundquist hosted a reception on the executive residence terrace for Drucilla "Drue" Smith, a longtime Capitol Hill reporter. Drue picked the date and the 150 invitees. They included four governors, members of the legislature, and state supreme court justices. Drue was honored with a proclamation by Governor Sundquist and heard laudatory remarks by Governors Dunn, Alexander, and McWherter.[10] The following summer Governor Sundquist reigned as King of the Bell Buckle, Tennessee, Moon Pie Festival. Who was his queen— none other than Drue Smith!

Five living Tennessee governors were together at the residence when the Sundquists hosted a luncheon for the Tennessee's Bicentennial on Statehood Day, June 1, 1996. The governors attending were Dunn, Blanton, Alexander, McWherter, and Sundquist. The Sundquists served as honorary chairmen of the year-long Bicentennial celebration.[11]

Whenever opportunities present themselves, the Sundquists enjoy inviting personal friends to the executive residence for meals and fellowship. That happened in July 1998 when Governor Sundquist invited an old congressional buddy, Republican Hal Rogers, of Somerset, Kentucky, to visit Nashville for a round of golf and a dinner party. At the time, Rogers was a sixty-one-year-old widower whose wife, Shirley, had died in 1995 after a long battle with cancer. Unknown to Rogers, Governor Sundquist had also invited Cynthia Stewart, a longtime political supporter of his, to the same party. Stewart was divorced and, like Rogers, had three grown children. During the evening, United States Representative Rogers and Mrs. Stewart enjoyed each other's company so much that they later began dating. The following New Year's Eve, at the executive residence, Rogers proposed to Stewart, who accepted. Governor Sundquist had set the scene by

Governor Sundquist giving candy-filled canes to children at the residence staff's annual holiday party. TPS

lighting a fire in the fireplace in his office and putting on some quiet romantic music. When Rogers proposed, Anne Murray's popular song, "Could I Have This Dance for the Rest of My Life?" was playing. The song was written by Waylon Holyfield, a friend of the Sundquists and Mrs. Stewart. The Rogers-Stewart nuptials took place on May 29, 1999, at the executive residence.[12]

A less pleasant episode began the summer of 1998 when Democratic gubernatorial candidate John Jay Hooker[13] filed a lawsuit over alleged illegal campaign fund-raising activities by Governor Sundquist. Hooker's position was that the governor

had used the State Capitol and the executive residence for fundraising and for other political activities and that state law, therefore, should provide him with "reasonably equal access" to those facilities for his own campaign. Hooker asked the court for a speedy issuance of a court order that would let him hold political rallies at the executive residence on October 17 and at the State Capitol on October 24. In unusually strong language, Davidson County Chancellor Ellen Hobbs Lyle said, on September 10, that Hooker and his lawyer Larry Woods should "put aside the posturing and 'hot air' and provide legal authority and analysis to justify and merit

Peacock door knocker at the executive residence, used by the Sundquists as a model for their commemorative pewter ornaments. TPS

their use of the legal system." In a written order, the chancellor said that she would not take any action on the lawsuit until Hooker or Woods presented some "shred of legal authority" to support Hooker's claim that he was entitled to use the State Capitol and the executive residence for campaign rallies. Governor Sundquist's spokeswoman, Beth Fortune, declined to comment on Hooker's lawsuit except to say, "Obviously, he likes to file lawsuits. This isn't the first time he has sued the governor."[14] The next day, Chancellor Lyle recused herself from the case because of a potential conflict of interest. Buoyed by this good news, Hooker, the following Saturday, delivered a colorful speech in which he compared himself with his friend, Muhammad Ali, whose famous heavyweight boxing match with Joe Frazier was dubbed "Thrilla in Manilla." Hooker said, while shadowboxing behind the podium, that he wanted to have "a hassle in the castle" with Governor Sundquist.[15] Ten days later, Davidson County Chancellor Irvin Kilcrease refused to allow Hooker to use Tennessee's executive residence

for a campaign rally, ruling that the governor and his staff were specifically exempt from a 1972 state law giving opposing candidates "reasonably equal access" to state buildings that are used for political purposes.[16] Despite having conducted a low-key campaign, Governor Sundquist was reelected governor of Tennessee in the general election on November 3, 1998. He received a record-breaking 68 percent of the vote, allowing him to focus on his agenda for his second term.

For Christmas 1998, the Sundquists decorated the executive residence with the help of Larry Keeton of Dick's Flowers in Donelson.[17] Mr. Keeton has donated the decorations plus his time and his employees for twenty years. Each window facing the front entrance featured a wreath with a red ribbon. A Christmas tree in the foyer was decorated by the Shelbyville branch of the Cheekwood Chapter of Embroiderers Guild of America. Additionally, a tree matching in size was placed in the living room. Mrs. Sundquist's extensive collection of nativity scenes and a display of the Heritage collection of Dickens' Christmas village, owned by Billy and Alma Ford, graced the entrance hall.[18] The first lady shared the beautifully decorated executive residence with the people of Tennessee by opening the house for visitors from 10:00 A.M. until noon on the first three days of December.[19]

Many friends of the governor and first lady look forward each Christmas to receiving a pewter Christmas ornament from the Sundquists. In 1998, the ornament was a facsimile of the angel statue in the reflecting pool. In previous years, the ornaments were miniature replicas of the State Capitol, the executive residence, and the peacock door knocker which had been made for the home's original owners, Mr. and Mrs. W. R. Wills. The ornaments are made by Tennessee Pewter Company of Grand Junction, Tennessee.

The Sundquists spent Christmas Day 1998 at the executive residence with their two daughters, Tania Williamson and Andrea Jeannet and their respective spouses, David and Art; also the Sundquists' granddaughter, Gabrielle Jeannet; their son, Donald K. "Deke" Sundquist Jr.; and Governor Sundquist's widowed mother, Louise Sundquist.

Governor Sundquist enjoyed hosting University of Tennessee coach Pat Summit and her NCAA-Division 1 National Championship Lady Vols at the executive residence. TPS

Deke Sundquist, Elizabeth Rochford, Art Jeannet, Gabrielle Jeannet, Andrea Sundquist Jeannet, Louise Sundquist, Don and Martha Sundquist, Tania Sundquist Williamson, and David Williamson. TPS

Sundquist granddaughter, Gabrielle, with mom Andrea Sundquist Jeannet at the 1999 inauguration. TPS

The Sundquists' two dogs, Millie and Ruby, are also part of each Sundquist Christmas. Deke, who moved to Nashville in 1998, was given his nickname in honor of the astronaut, Deke Slayton. As his sisters did, Deke Sundquist helped in Governor Sundquist's 1998 reelection campaign and also with the planning for his father's second inauguration on January 16, 1999. Today, the Williamsons live in Charlotte, North Carolina; Jeannets' home is in Phoenix, Arizona.

In recalling the countless receptions, dinners, and special events held at the executive residence, Mrs. Sundquist, in 1998, commented that these events would not come off so efficiently and smoothly without a strong staff which includes Alma and Billy Ford, who manage the residence, and Anne Locke, Mrs. Sundquist's administrative assistant.[20] In order to entertain as extensively as the Sundquists do, there has to be a strong support staff.

For parties and receptions, such as when former President George Bush visited the Sundquists on December 5, 1997, Mrs. Sundquist depends on an approved list of Nashville caterers. Before that particular visit, the Secret Service temporarily sealed up one of the two doors to the guest bedroom where President Bush slept. Earlier, on August 24, 1996, Vice President and Mrs. Dan Quayle were overnight guests at the executive residence. They were in Nashville

Deke Sundquist enjoyng playing with the family pets, Millie and Ruby. TPS

One of the many dinners hosted in the formal dining room of the executive residence by Governor and Mrs. Sundquist. TPS

because their daughter was a student at Vanderbilt University.

Three cooks prepare food for approximately twenty staff members daily and for the Sundquists, when they are there without company. The senior cook is Ida Finch, who has worked in the kitchen at the executive residence since the Alexander administration. The other two are Vicki Nelson and Jennie White. On those relatively infrequent occasions when the Sundquists dine alone, they normally eat very simply. For lunch, they are likely to have pimiento cheese or bacon, lettuce, and tomato sandwiches in the Greeneville Room. Martha Sundquist, who is quite thin, admits that she keeps her weight in line by eating only half portions or half a sandwich. Vicki Nelson once joked that "Mrs. Sundquist likes her food half-sized and half-done."

The Sundquists acquired, in 1998, six handsome reproduction Windsor chairs for the Greeneville Room. The chairs were made by skilled Greeneville craftsman Bill Showalter. The Sundquists' everyday dishes were made by Tennessee potter Alan Monsarrat.

Although the house staff members are professionals employed by the state, some members of the work crew on the grounds are prisoners from Tennessee State Prison. Once a prisoner working there as a painter mentioned to the first lady that his nine-year-old son's schoolmates did not believe him when he said that his dad worked at the executive residence. The man, who was in prison for murder, asked if Governor Sundquist would write the boy a note confirming that his dad actually worked there. The governor wrote the youngster on the boy's birthday and said, "By the way, your father is doing a great job." Later, Governor Sundquist took the time to visit the elementary school the boy attended in a Middle Tennessee town. He did not tell the other students why he came.[21]

One of the best workers at the executive residence during Governor Sundquist's first term was another prisoner convicted of murder. This model prisoner was the best gardener at the residence and a thoughtful person. Often he would bring little wood carvings as gifts for Mrs. Sundquist. In time Governor Sundquist commuted his sentence, after which the man continued to work as a gardener at the executive residence. Sadly, he left without notice.[22]

The work outside is supervised by a full-time horticulturist, John Wilson. Mrs. Sundquist, who enjoys being outside and loves gardening, said, "He does the serious stuff, such as fertilizing and weeding, while I pick roses to bring in the house, add a few plants, and pick stray weeds his staff has missed." In the summers, on days when visitors are not around, the first lady sometimes puts on her swim suit and climbs in the reflecting pool to clean out the dead water lily leaves. She particularly enjoys the rose garden, which was renovated by the Nashville Rose Society in anticipation for the annual meeting of the American Rose Society held in Nashville in May 1999.[23]

Martha Sundquist continues to utilize her interests, energy, and abilities to benefit Tennessee and Tennesseans. Hopefully, one of the gifts she will be remembered for will be the publication of this book. She wanted it published so that those Tennesseans who have not had an opportunity to visit the executive residence will be able to see color photographs of and enjoy reading about the handsome interior decorations, furniture, and memorabilia, of the residence and to vicariously experience what the lives of our first families were like through anecdotes and stories. By stepping back in time to include stories about Tennessee's two earlier executive residences, this book represents a social history of the lives of Tennessee's chief executives and their families from 1907 through 1999, spanning almost the entire twentieth century.

PART THREE
TENNESSEE EXECUTIVE RESIDENCE

ABOVE: East elevation, 1996. TPS

OPPOSITE: West elevation, 1984. TPS

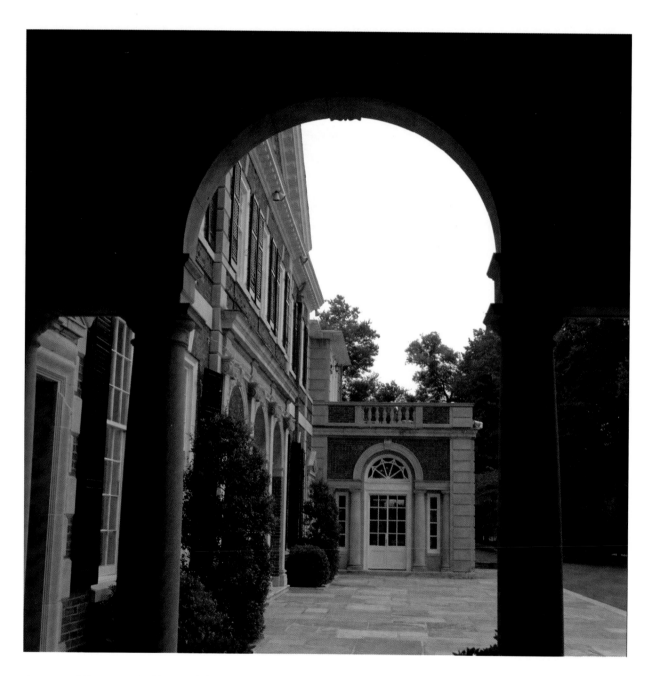

ABOVE and OPPOSITE: Architectural detail, west elevation, 1996. TPS

Formal living room, 1996.TPS

Sitting room, 1996. TPS

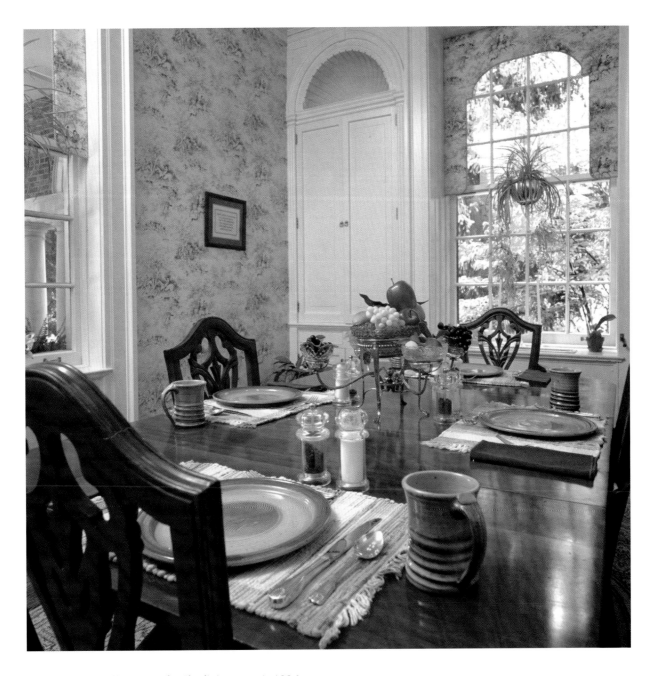

Above: Greeneville Room (family dining room), 1996. TPS

Opposite: Formal dining room, 1996. TPS

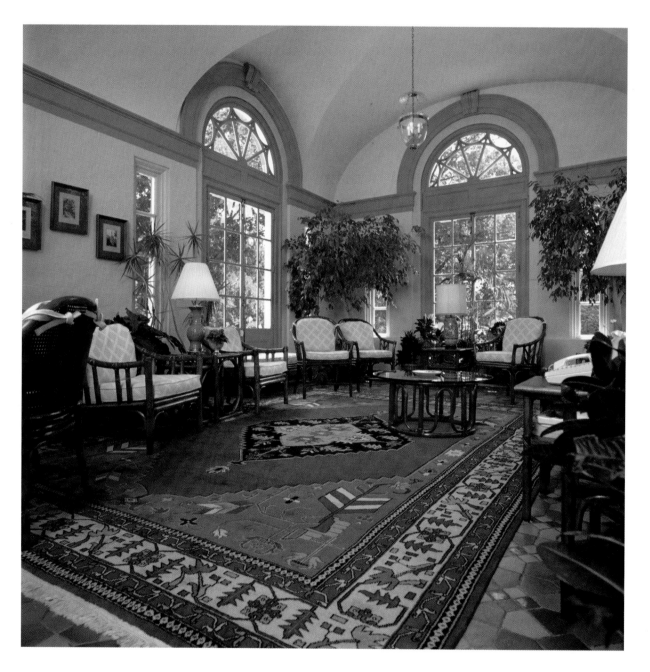

ABOVE: Sun room, 1996. TPS

OPPOSITE: Foyer, 1996. TPS

East elevation, 1996. TPS

Pool and pool house, 1996. TPS

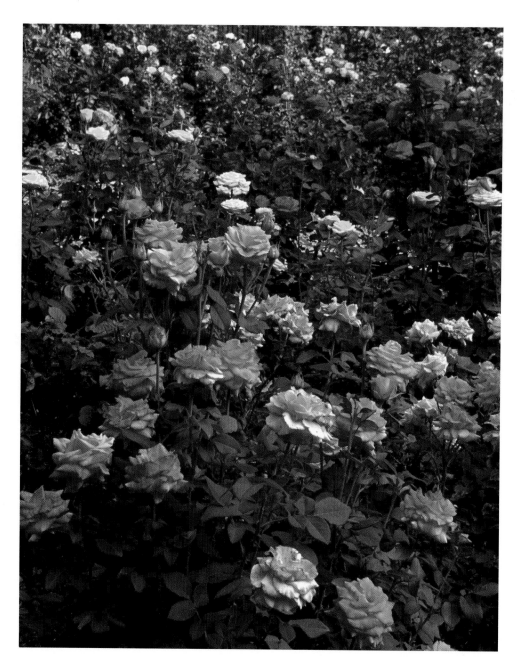

ABOVE: Rose garden, 1999. TPS

OPPOSITE: Lily pond with angel statue, 1998. TPS

NOTES

Chapter One

1. Betsy Beeler Creekmore, *Knoxville* (Knoxville: University of Tennessee Press, 1958), 75.

2. James A. Crutchfield, ed., *The Tennessee Almanac and Book of Facts*, 1989–1990, 178.

3. Ibid., 178–79.

4. In September 1894, Judge John H. Henderson, of Franklin, noted in his journal (p. 255) that, "While at Knoxville, I visited the house at which the first legislature of Tennessee was held."

5. C. C. Henderson, *The Story of Murfreesboro* (Murfreesboro: The News-Banner Publishing Co., 1929), 41.

6. *Tennessee House Journal, 28th Assembly, 1849–50*, 536.

7. *Harper's Weekly*, March 8, 1862, 153.

8. Ed Huddleston, "Asylum Site Skipped for Governor Mansion," *Nashville Banner*, October 11, 1961.

9. Louise Douglas, "Other Wartime Holidays Are Recalled as Yuletide Draws Near," *Nashville Banner*, December 23, 1942.

10. The Campbell house had been built by the former United States Senator George Washington Campbell (1769–1848) in 1843 when he sold his earlier home on Cedar Knob to the State of Tennessee as the site for the State Capitol. Waymouth T. Jordan, *George Washington Campbell of Tennessee, Western Statesman* (Tallahassee: Florida State University, 1955), 197–98.

11. Louise Davis, "Housing a Governor," *Nashville Tennessean* Magazine, January 2, 1949, 6 (hereafter cited as Davis, "Housing a Governor").

12. *Messages of the Governors of Tennessee 1883–1899*, vol. 7, Tennessee Historical Commission (Nashville: Benson Printing Co., 1967), 342–43.

Chapter Two

1. *Acts of Tennessee, 55th Assembly, 1907*, chap. 38, 131–32.

2. Mr. and Mrs. Williams built the house in 1890 at a cost of $60,000. George W. Thompson and Henry Gibel were the architects. Allen Morrison, *The City of Nashville* (St. Louis, George W. Engelhardt Co., 1892), 72–73.

3. Louise Davis, "Governor's Mansions Echo with History— Love, War, Scandal," *Nashville Tennessean*, sec. F, July 9, 1999.

4. Morgan Reynolds, *Seventy Years of Belle Meade Country Club* (Nashville: McQuiddy Printing Co., 1971), 1.

5. Polk Place was bounded by Spring Street on the south, North Spruce Street on the west, Union Street on the north, and North Vine Street on the east.

6. *Tennessee Historical Quarterly* (spring 1959): 28–29.

7. Davis, "Housing a Governor," 6.

8. John P. Williams's wife, Elizabeth "Lizzie" Cheney Williams, was the granddaughter of Samuel Dold Morgan, chairman of the committee that designed and erected the Tennessee State Capitol.

9. Jesse Overton Colton, conversation with author, March 9, 1998.

10. William Waller, *Nashville in the 1890s* (Nashville: Vanderbilt University Press, 1970), 313.

11. *Union City (Tenn.) Commercial*, December 13, 1907.

12. Mary Gardner Patterson Phillips interview by author, Memphis, Tenn., December 15, 1997.

13. Mary Gardner Patterson Phillips remembered being told by her parents that they went to Niagara Falls on their honeymoon. *Union City (Tenn.) Commercial*, December 13, 1907.

14. *Nashville Banner*, October 22, 1907.

15. Josiah Patterson and his son, Malcolm Patterson, occupied the same seat in congress from Tennessee's Tenth District.

16. When appointed to the Civil Service Commission by President Franklin Roosevelt in 1933, Mrs. McMillin occupied the highest public office ever held by a woman in the United States.

17. *Nashville American*, November 10, 1907.

18. Ibid.

19. Margaret Phillips, *The Governors of Tennessee* (Gretna: Pelican Publishing Co., 1978), 125 (hereafter cited as Phillips, *Governors of Tennessee*).

20. *Nashville Banner*, September 25, 1908.

21. Everett Robert Boyce, ed., *The Unwanted Boy: The Autobiography of Governor Ben W. Hooper* (Knoxville: University of Tennessee Press, 1963), 95 (hereafter cited as Boyce, *The Unwanted Boy*).

22. Davis, "Housing a Governor."

23. *Nashville Banner*, Nov. 25, 1916.

24. Boyce, *The Unwanted Boy*, 96.

25. *Nashville Banner*, September 20, 1911.

26. The Hooper children and their years of birth were Anna B. (1902), Ben Jones (1904), James Randolph (1906), Margaret (1909), Lemuel Washington (1911), and Newell Sanders (1916).

27. Boyce, *The Unwanted Boy*, 243.

28. Ibid., 161.

29. *Nashville Tennessean*, September 13, 1953.

30. Thomas C. Rye was the last Tennessee governor to be elected by a convention.

31. *Nashville Tennessean*, September 13, 1953.

32. *Nashville Banner*, October 16, 1916.

33. Ibid.

34. The Ryes' daughter, Nell, was married to John F. Nolan, of Nashville, who served as chief clerk of the state comptroller and later as state treasurer.

35. Mrs. John F. Caldwell Jr., conversation with author, December 17, 1998 (hereafter cited as Caldwell, conversation). Mrs. Caldwell is a granddaughter of Governor and Mrs. Rye.

36. *Nashville Tennessean* Magazine, March 2, 1946.

37. *Nashville Tennessean*, September 13, 1953.

38. Caldwell, conversation.

39. *Nashville Tennessean*, September 13, 1953.

40. *Nashville Tennessean* Magazine, March 2, 1946.

41. Ibid.

42. *Nashville Tennessean*, October 23, 1961.

43. John Perry, *Sgt. York: His Life, Legend and Legacy* (Nashville: Broadman & Holman Publishers, 1997), 124 (hereafter cited as Perry, *Sgt. York*).

44. Sam K. Cowan, *Sergeant York* (New York: Grosset & Dunlap, 1922), 280 (hereafter cited as Cowan, *Sergeant York*).
45. Perry, *Sgt. York*, 130.
46. Cowan, *Sergeant York*, 281–82.
47. Davis, "Housing a Governor."
48. Kenneth S. Braden, "The Wizard of Overton, Governor A. H. Roberts of Tennessee," (thesis, Memphis State University, 1983), 112–13, 177.
49. Mary Louise Lea Tidwell, *Luke Lea of Tennessee* (Bowling Green, Ohio: Bowling Green State University Popular Press, 1993), 151.

Chapter Three

1. The Taylors' second oldest son, Benjamin Harrison Taylor, was married and practicing law in Johnson City when his father was elected governor. In 1921, Ben's wife, Lela Ramsey Taylor, gave birth to their first child, a daughter, Jennie. Benjamin Harrison Taylor Jr., conversation with author, November 22, 1998.
2. Florence Taylor Greer, conversation with author, October 26, 1998.
3. Landon Taylor, conversation with author, October 25, 1998.
4. Carter Williams Jr., M.D., conversation with author, October 29, 1998.
5. Robert Love Taylor Jr., conversation with author, October 25, 1998.
6. "Mrs. Caldwell Makes Plea for Preservation of Historic Buildings," from an undated Nashville newspaper in the collection of author.
7. The Farrell family sold Burlington, which was adjacent to Centennial Park, to the Catholic Diocese of Tennessee in 1928. Burlington was razed and Father Ryan High School opened on the site in the fall of 1929. Thomas Stritch, *The Catholic Church in Tennessee: The Sesquicentennial Story* (Nashville: The Catholic Center, 1987), 310.
8. Davis, "Housing a Governor."
9. Leslie Cheek and his wife, Mabel Wood Cheek, built, beginning in 1929, a fifty-room mansion just outside Nashville called "Cheekwood."
10. *Nashville Tennessean*, February 27, 1977.
11. *Austin Peay, Governor of Tennessee, 1923–1927, A Collection of State Papers and Public Addresses with a Biography by T. H. Alexander* (Kingsport: Southern Publishers, 1929), 417.
12. Ibid., xxii.
13. Ibid., 440.
14. Charlotte A. Williams, comp., *The Centennial Club of Nashville: A History from 1905–77* (Nashville: Centennial Club, 1978), 151 (hereafter cited as Williams, *Centennial Club*).
15. Judge Joel B. Fort, address, Memorial Service for Governor Austin Peay, Edgefield Baptist Church, Nashville, October 9, 1927.
16. Austin Peay, *Governor of Tennessee*, 244.
17. Phillips, *Governors of Tennessee*, 143.
18. T. H. Alexander III, "T. H. Alexander—Southern Columnist," *Williamson County Historical Journal* 29 (1998): 97.
19. "Governor's Granddaughter Buys First Christmas Seal in County," *Nashville Banner*, November 25, 1928.
20. *Nashville Tennessean*, July 3, 1939.
21. *Fayetteville Lincoln County News*, July 5, 1934.
22. I. D. Beasley, Jim Cummings, and Walter "Pete" Haynes were called by their political enemies the "Unholy Trinity." For many years this triumvirate controlled the Tennessee state legislature in the interests of the rural areas of the state. Lee Seifert Greene, *Lead Me On: Frank Goad Clement and Tennessee Politics* (Knoxville: University of Tennessee Press, 1982), 173 (hereafter cited as Greene, *Lead Me On*).
23. J. C. McMurtry, *Humor in Tennessee Justice* (Tompkinsville, Ky.: Monroe County Press, 1979), 288–89 (hereafter cited as McMurtry, *Humor in Tennessee Justice*).
24. *Nashville Tennessean*, July 3, 1939.
25. Louise Jackson McAlister was the daughter of Judge Howell and Mary Harding Jackson. At the time of his death in 1895, Judge Jackson was an associate justice on the United States Supreme Court and had earlier served as a United States senator from Tennessee.
26. Nashville newspaper, April 1932.
27. Donald U. Bathrick Jr., grandson of Governor and Mrs. McAlister, conversation with author, June 16, 1998.
28. Hill McAlister Papers, Tennessee State Library and Archives, Nashville.
29. *Nashville Tennessean*, November 1, 1959.
30. *Nashville Banner*, February 2, 1941.

31. McMurtry, *Humor in Tennessee Justice*, 250–51.

32. Williams, *Centennial Club of Nashville*, 355.

33. After graduating from Webb School, where he distinguished himself in oratory, Prentice Cooper attended Vanderbilt University. He transferred to Princeton for his junior year. There he won the declamation contest. After graduating from Princeton in 1917, he went into military service during World War I.

34. William Prentice Cooper Sr. was a lawyer and president of the Peoples National Bank of Shelbyville. He was a member of Tennessee's fifty-ninth General Assembly and speaker of the house in 1915.

35. Cooper, then district governor of the Rotary Club, was in Europe to attend a Rotary International meeting with his parents.

36. Margaret Sloan, conversation with author, January 20, 1999 (hereafter cited as Sloan, conversation).

37. Thomas H. Hudson, interview by author, December 12, 1997. The Hudsons also invited the governor to a fraternity dance at the Belle Meade Country Club.

38. Governor Cooper drew plans for four handsome crab orchard stone buildings in Shelbyville, then supervised and worked on their construction.

39. An oil portrait Governor Cooper painted of his mother, Argie Shofner Cooper, still hangs in the parlor of his homeplace in Shelbyville.

40. Phillips, *Governors of Tennessee*, 159.

41. Ibid., 158.

42. *Nashville Banner*, May 14, 1944.

43. *Marshall County, Tennessee, A Sesquicentennial History*, 159; *Nashville Tennessesean*, January 30, 1945.

44. *Nashville Tennessean*, August 6, 1944.

45. Ibid.

46. *Nashville Banner*, May 14, 1944.

47. Editorial, *The Lookout*, 1953.

48. *Nashville Banner*, October 8, 1948.

49. In 1947, Roy O. Elam's Dental Clinic was at 2102 West End. The United States Engineers occupied 2110 West End. Dr. Lucius E. Burch and his partners, Dr. Richard E. Strain and Dr. James L. Pinkston, operated the Burch Clinic at 2112 West End. The Kappa Alpha Theta Sorority was at 2114 and a medical clinic, where Drs. Oval N. Bryan, Scott Bayer, Hollis E. Johnson, and David W. Strayhorn Jr. practiced, was at 2122 West End.

50. Davis, "Housing a Governor."

51. Mrs. McCord was the daughter of W. K. and Mollie Kercheval, of Lewisburg, Tennessee. It was in partnership with Mr. Kercheval that Jim McCord purchased the *Marshall Gazette* in 1910. Two years later, he bought out his father-in-law's interest and became owner and publisher of the newspaper. James C. McCord Papers, Biographical Sketch, Tennessee State Library and Archives, Nashville.

52. Phillips, *Governors of Tennessee*, 159–60.

Chapter Four

1. This story was told Governor Ned Ray McWherter by Seth Norman, a good friend of Governor Browning.

2. Legislator Dave Alexander Sr. proposed the legislation that authorized the purchase of an executive residence for the State of Tennessee. Mike Pigott, "Current Governor's Home Result of Long Search," *Nashville Banner*, May 14, 1984., sec. B.

3. The state committee included former Governor Jim McCord, Secretary of State Joe Carr, Finance and Taxation Commissioner Sam Carson, State Treasurer J. F. Murrey, Attorney General Roy H. Beeler, and Comptroller Jared Maddux.

4. Ridley Wills had been, since 1936, incompetent to handle his affairs, suffering from a severe depression. *Register's Book 669*, 55; *Book 700*, 143, 513, 701, Register's Office, Davidson County, Tennessee.

5. Other contractors were Nashville Floor Laying Co., Keith-Simmons Co., and E. P. Scales Engineering Co. M. S. Roberts to W. R. Wills, letter, March 11, 1931, in collection of author.

6. Jesse E. Wills, "Memoirs of Far Hills," June 14, 1971, copy in the collection of author.

7. For Christmas 1997, Governor and Mrs. Don Sundquist sent friends pewter Christmas ornaments each of which was a replica of the original Wills door knockers at Far Hills. The ornaments were handcrafted by Tennessee artisans at the Tennessee Pewter Company, Grand Junction, Tennessee.

8. The executive residence has seventeen rooms, exclusive of bathrooms, wardrobes, and closets. It contains approximately ten thousand square feet of usable space on three floors.

9. Certificate No. 1530, issued by Hart, Freeland & Roberts Architects, March 11, 1931, copy in the collection of the author.

10. Recollections of friends, such as Peggy Henry, who attended the birthday parties.

11. Andrew B. Benedict Jr., interview by author, February 7, 1998.

12. *Nashville Tennessean*, April 1, 1949.

13. *Tennessee Historical Quarterly*, 38, no. 3, (fall 1979): 377.

14. Benedict, interview.

15. *Nashville Tennessean*, October 12, 14, 1949.

16. *Nashville Tennessean*, May 24, 1976.

Chapter Five

1. *Knoxville News-Sentinel*, June 15, 1980.

2. Greene, *Lead Me On*, 85.

3. Mary Smith, Governor Clement's personal secretary, interview by author, February 14, 1998 (hereafter cited as Smith, interview).

4. "Frank Goad Clement and the Keynote Address of 1956," *Tennessee Historical Quarterly*, 36, no. 1 (spring 1977): 97.

5. Ibid., 101.

6. Sloan, conversation.

7. Mary Follin, conversation with author, January 22, 1999.

8. Greene, *Lead Me On*, 225.

9. Ibid., 238; Albert Gore, *Let the Glory Out: My South and Its Politics*

(New York: The Viking Press, 1972), 90.

10. Congressman Bob Clement, interview by author, August 20, 1998 (hereafter cited as Bob Clement, interview).

11. Ibid.

12. Benedict, interview.

13. Frank G. Clement Jr., interview by author, February 6, 1998 (hereafter cited as Frank Clement, interview).

14. Ibid., 273.

15. *Nashville Tennessean*, August 2, 1962.

16. Mrs. Ellington was assisted in paying household bills by her secretary, Miss Lily Clemons. *Memphis Commercial-Appeal*, December 3, 1961.

17. Lamar Alexander, *Six Months Off: An American Family's Australian Adventure* (New York: William Morrow and Company, 1988), 22 (hereafter cited as Alexander, *Six Months Off*).

18. Ann Ellington Wagner, interview by author, February 18, 1998.

19. *Nashville Tennessean*, August 2, 1962.

20. Robert N. Moore Jr., letter to author, January 30, 1998.

21. *Nashville Tennessean*, December 20, 1961.

22. "Widow of Former Governor Ellington Dies," *Nashville Tennessean*, December 23, 1998.

23. Bob Clement, interview.

24. Greene, *Lead Me On*, 288–89.

25. Benedict, interview. The next day, many of the children saw their picture in the *Nashville Tennessean*.

26. Eddie Jones, interview by author, February 10, 1998.

27. Governor Clement gave the pres-

ident a copy of Andrew Johnson's "Messages" to the legislature. The president reciprocated by giving the governor an autographed picture of Clark Mills's statue of Andrew Jackson across from the White House and a paragraph from Andrew Jackson's farewell address to Congress. *Nashville Tennessean*, May 19, 1963.

28. Ibid.

29. Thomas E. Nesbitt, M.D., interview by author, October 21, 1998.

30. Frank Clement, interview.

31. Smith, interview. Governor Clement was known to visit condemned prisoners on death row and their families. According to Ms. Smith, he agonized, cried, and prayed over his decisions regarding overturning their death sentences.

32. "Widow of Former Governor Ellington Dies," *Nashville Tennessean*, December 23, 1998.

33. *Knoxville News-Sentinel*, June 15, 1980.

34. *Nashville Banner*, March 15, 1967.

35. Andrew Jackson was born on the fifteenth of March 1767. James Parton, *Life of Andrew Jackson in Three Volumes*, vol. 1, (New York: Mason Brothers, 1860), 52.

36. *Nashville Tennessean*, March 16, 1967.

37. Dave Alexander Jr., M.D., conversation with author, June 23, 1998.

38. When Governor Ellington's widow, Anna Catherine Cheek Ellington, died in December 1998, her family asked that memorial gifts be made to the Agricultural Museum at the Ellington Agricultural Center.

Chapter Six

1. This was the first time that the Tennessee executive residence was officially opened to the public on a regular basis.

2. The incorporators of the Executive Residence Preservation Foundation were Mrs. Cecil Rogan Allen, Ward DeWitt Jr., Mrs. Winfield Dunn, Roupen M. Gulbenk, Stanley F. Horn, Robert N. McBride, Owen N. Meredith, David Steine, and David K. Wilson, all of Nashville; and Mrs. Park Niceley, of Knoxville.

3. *Tennessee Historical Quarterly*, 30, no. 2 (summer 1971): 216.

4. The silver bowl and cups had been originally presented to the armored cruiser *Tennessee* in 1906. The set was transferred to the battleship USS *Tennessee* in 1920.

5. "Governor's Mansion Brochure," Dunn Administration, 11.

6. Betty (Mrs. Winfield) Dunn, interview by author, August 18, 1998.

7. Ibid., March 15, 1998.

8. Governor and Mrs. Winfield Dunn, interview by author, June 19, 1998.

9. Alf and Peggy Adams, Dortch and Sis Oldham, and Lee and Billie Ann Smith were also guests at the party.

10. Mrs. Winfield Dunn's written reminiscence, June 23, 1998.

Chapter Seven

1. Mrs. Pruitt, Tennessee Commissioner of General Services, interview by author, *Nashville Banner*, July 11, 1979.

2. Alexander, *Six Months Off*, 24.

3. Betty Blanton, interview by author, February 16, 1998 (hereafter cited as B. Blanton, interview).

4. *Nashville Tennessean*, December 12, 1975.

5. Ibid., December 14, 1975.

6. President Nimeiri was the first black man to attend the Swan Ball.

7. B. Blanton, interview.

8. Deborah Blanton Flack, conversation with author, February 19, 1999.

9. Edward G. Nelson, interview by author, February 17, 1998.

10. Present at the dinner, in addition to Governor and Mrs. Blanton, were Governor Blanton's parents, Mr. and Mrs. Leonard Blanton; his brother Gene's wife, Jimmy Wayne Blanton; the governor's children, Debbie, David, and Paul; and Debbie's husband, Lewis Flack III.

11. The United Nations Ambassadorial Corps was invited to Nashville by Dr. Pearl Bailey, a Vanderbilt University professor who was president of the United Nations Association chapter in Nashville.

12. B. Blanton, interview.

13. Gertrude Butler, telephone conversation with author, February 23, 1998.

14. *Knoxville News-Sentinel*, June 15, 1980.

15. *Nashville Banner*, July 4, 1977.

16. Ibid., May 19, 1976.

17. Ibid., July 4, 1977.

18. The other donors were Stratton Foster and Mr. and Mrs. Roupen Gulbenk, all of Nashville, and Mrs. Park Niceley, of Knoxville.

19. The Diego Cisneros family of Caracas were sponsors of the Venezuelan Friendship Force.

Chapter Eight

1. Alexander, *Six Months Off*, 60–63.

2. Lamar Alexander, *Steps along the Way: A Governor's Scrapbook* (Nashville: Thomas Nelson Publishers, 1986), 65 (hereafter cited as Alexander, *Steps along the Way*).

3. *Memphis Commercial-Appeal*, July 5, 1981.

4. Ibid., March 9, 1980.

5. *Architectural Digest*, December 1985.

6. There had been eighteen minimum security prison inmates, who earned no pay, assigned to the executive residence during the last months of the Blanton administration. They cooked, cleaned the house, and maintained the grounds.

7. Alexander, *Six Months Off*, 24.

8. Ibid.

9. Carol (Mrs. Roy) Elam, conversation with author, October 6, 1998.

10. Lemuel Washington Hooper, son of Governor and Mrs. Ben Hooper, was born August 6, 1911, during his father's first year as governor of Tennessee.

11. *Chattanooga News-Free Press*, November 4, 1979.

12. Ibid., September 17, 1979.

13. *Nashville Tennessean*, October 7, 1979.

14. *Nashville Banner*, March 16, 1979.

15. Mr. Colorio resigned his employment in August 1980.

16. Ida Finch, conversation with

author, December 10, 1998 (hereafter cited as Finch, conversation).

17. *Nashville Banner*, September 17, 1979.

18. The projected cost of operating the Tennessee executive residence for the fiscal year beginning July 1, 1979, was $261,000. This compared with the approximately $240,000 spent in fiscal year 1978.

19. *Nashville Banner*, December 10, 1979. The staff consisted of four custodians, one gardener, two food service supervisors, and three yard helpers.

20. *Nashville Banner*, March 14, 1980.

21. Ibid., March 3, 1980.

22. *Memphis Commercial-Appeal*, March 9, 1980.

23. Ibid., July 5, 1981.

24. *Nashville Banner*, December 5, 1980. Davis Cabinet Company was the third party participating in the gift to the executive residence.

25. *Chattanooga News-Free Press*, June 15, 1980; *Nashville Tennessean*, June 22, 1980.

26. Governor Alexander's chair depicted the state symbols—the native iris, mockingbird, and tulip poplar sapling. Mrs. Alexander's chair showed the dogwood and bluejay.

27. The expense of the needlepoint project was a gift from the Sam M. Fleming and Toby Wilt families of Nashville.

28. *Chattanooga News-Free Press*, December 1980.

29. A portrait of Tennessee's first governor, John Sevier, had been moved to the dining room.

30. *Chattanooga News Free-Press*, May 17, 1981.

31. *Knoxville News-Sentinel*, May 10, 1981.

32. Ibid. Drew was an avid baseball fan. He enjoyed playing soccer, baseball, basketball, and ice hockey. All the children enjoyed riding their bikes and their horse, Buddy. *Chattanooga News-Free Press*, November 4, 1979.

33. Knoxville New-Sentinel, May 10, 1981.

34. Chattanooga News Free Press, May 17, 1981.

35. Richard Doughty, of Greeneville, headed the committee that selected the furnishings for the room. Governor and Mrs. Alexander hosted a luncheon for Mr. Doughty and the other donors prior to the room's official opening. *Greeneville Sun*, June 17, 1981.

36. *Knoxville News-Sentinel*, May 10, 1981.

37. Leslee and Kathryn shared a bedroom so that there would be a guest bedroom available. As part of the bargain, they got twin canopied beds. *Chattanooga Times*, August 1, 1981.

38. John Austin Echols received the "most-frequent-visitor-at-the governor's residence award." In his book, *Steps along the Way*, Governor Alexander wrote that John Austin and Will Alexander gave the "Children Playing" sign at the driveway some real meaning.

39. Jean Searcy, interview by author, February 14, 1998.

40. *Nashville Banner*, May 8, 1981; *Memphis Commercial-Appeal*, July 5, 1981.

41. Alexander, *Steps along the Way*, 100.

42. Alexander, *Six Months Off*, 95.

43. Governor Lamar Alexander Farewell Address, January 14, 1987.

Chapter Nine

1. Walter G. Knestrick, conversation with author, October 6, 1998.

2. While he was governor, Ned McWherter's interest in Volunteer Distributing, Inc. in Dresden, Tennessee, and Central Distributors in Jackson, Tennessee, was held in trust. His son, Mike McWherter, ran Central Distributors in partnership with the trust until his father left office.

3. Finch, conversation.

4. "McWherter is Honorary Head of Cancer Fund-raising Group," *Nashville Banner*, January 12, 1988.

5. David D. Dortch, conversation with author, February 28, 1998.

6. McWherter's daughter, Linda Ramsey, is married to Steve Ramsey. While her father was governor, the Ramseys lived in Martin, Tennessee, with their two children, Brett and Matt. Linda was then an associate professor in the Department of Physical Education at the University of Tennessee, Martin. Mike McWherter married Mary Jane Wooten of Covington, Tennessee, in 1989. They have two children, Walker, born in 1991, and Mary Bess, born in 1993.

7. Henry Cannon enjoyed telling this story to friends.

8. Governor Ned Ray McWherter, interview by author, September 24, 1998 (hereafter cited as Governor McWherter, interview).

9. Henry Cannon had once been a pilot for Hank Williams.

10. There are four original copies of the Magna Carta which still survive. In 1974, two copies were owned by the British Museum, one copy was in the Cathedral at Salisbury, and one copy was in the Lincoln Cathedral. *World Book Encyclopedia* (Chicago: Field Enterprises Educational Corp., 1974), 49.

11. Geoffrey Lewis, *Lord Hailsham* (London: Jonathan Cape, 1997), 9–10.

12. Governor McWherter, interview.

13. Ibid.

14. Michael R. McWherter, conversation with author, September 9, 1998 (hereafter cited as Michael McWherter, conversation).

15. Governor McWherter, interview.

16. Michael McWherter, interview by author, September 2, 1998.

17. Ibid.

18. Ibid., September 9, 1998.

19. Ibid.

20. Frank Clement, interview.

21. Peaches Simpkins was chairperson of the Tennessee Higher Education Commission under Governor McWherter. She also became a member of Governor Don Sundquist's cabinet. Peaches Simpkins served as deputy to the governor/chief of staff.

22. Irby Simpkins, conversation with author, June 24, 1998.

Chapter Ten

1. Members of the Tennessee Executive Residence Foundation in 1997 were Richard Deaderick, Knoxville; Richard Doughty, Greeneville; Roupen M. Gulbenk, Nashville, chairman; Mrs. James Haslam, Knoxville; Mary Henderson, Nashville; Owen Meredith, Nashville, secretary; Will Montague, Lookout Mountain; Mrs. Park Niceley, Knoxville; Martha Sundquist, Nashville, ex-officio; James Vaden, M.D., Cookeville; and David K. Wilson, Nashville.

2. Martha (Mrs. Don) Sundquist, interview by author, April 10, 1999 (hereafter cited as Martha Sundquist, interview).

3. Ibid., November 30, 1998.

4. Jan-Ojvind Swahn, *Maypoles, Crawfish and Lucia: Swedish Holidays and Traditions* (Stockholm: Jan-Ojvind Swahn and the Swedish Institute, 1994), 36–37.

5. Martha Sundquist, interview, November 30, 1998.

6. Martha Sundquist, interview, April 10, 1999.

7. Martha Sundquist, interview, November 30, 1998.

8. In 1995, Tennessee First Lady Martha Sundquist wrote the introduction to Netherton's book, *Tennessee: A Bicentennial Celebration.*

9. Martha Sundquist, interview, November 30, 1998.

10. Drue Smith, conversation with author, July 15, 1998.

11. Martha Sundquist, interview, April 10, 1999.

12. Ibid.

13. Before the 1998 gubernatorial campaign, John Jay Hooker ran unsuccessfully for governor of Tennessee in 1966 and 1971 and unsuccessfully for the United States Senate in 1976 and 1994.

14. "Hooker Suit Lacks Merit, Judge Says" *Nashville Tennessean,* September 11, 1998.

15. "Hooker Ready to 'Hassle' Sundquist," *Nashville Tennessean,* September 13, 1998.

16. "Ruling Ruins Hooker Rally Plan," *Nashville Tennessean,* September 22, 1998.

17. Larry Keeton also decorated the Tennessee executive residence for Christmas during the last two years of the Alexander administration and for all of the Blanton administration.

18. Billy and Alma Ford were the executive residence managers in 1999 and for many years before that.

19. *Green Hills News,* December 3, 1998.

20. Martha Sundquist, interview, December 17, 1998.

21. Martha Sundquist, interview, November 30, 1998.

22. Ibid.

23. Governor and Mrs. Don Sundquist, interview by author, December 17, 1998.

INDEX

Illustration page numbers are in **bold type.**

Clark, Mamie Craig. *See* Crook, Mamie Craig
Clark, Phoebe, xi; **xi**
Clarkston Hotel, 40
Claussen, Peter, 94
Clay, John, Jr., 111
Clay, Mrs. John, Jr., 111
Clement, Erma, 119
Clement, Frank G., 48, 59, 61–65, 68–75, 90; **58, 60–64, 71**
Clement, Frank G., Jr., 61, 63–65, 69–72, 118; **61, 64**
Clement, Gary, 61, 65, 72; **61, 64**
Clement, Jennifer, 119
Clement, Lucille (Mrs. Frank G.), 61–63, 69–72; **61, 64**
Clement, Robert N. "Bob," 61, 63–65, 69–71; **61, 64**
Clements, C. Runcie, 57
Clements, Mrs. Runcie C., 57
Clinton, Hillary Rodham, 115–116; **113**
Clinton, William Jefferson, 115–116; **113**
Cockerham, Mrs. Perry, 105
Collie, Mark, 127
Colorio, Anthony, 101
Columbia, Tenn., 17, 73, 122
Columbia State Community College, 73
Cone, Tom, 111
Cone, Mrs. Tom, 111
Cooper, Argie Shofner (Mrs. William Prentice, Sr.), 42, 45; **44**
Cooper, Duncan B., 16
Cooper, Hortense Hayes Powell (Mrs. Prentice), 45–46; **127**
Cooper, James H. S., 46
Cooper, John N. P., 46
Cooper, Prentice, 42–46; **43–45**
Cooper, William Prentice, Sr., 42
Cooper, William P., III, 46
Cosby, Tenn., 62
Cosner, Charlie, 40
Cox, John, 9
Crab Orchard, Tenn., 99
Criddle, C. B., 51, 53; **52**
Crook, George Wills, xi
Crook, Mamie Craig, xi–xii, 55
Crook, Senter C., xi
Crossville, Tenn., 26, 101
Crump, Edward H., 51

C. T. Cheek and Company, 33
Cumberland University, 87
Cummings, Mrs. James, 55
Cummings, Jim, 52
Cummings, Thomas L., 56
Cummings, Mrs. Thomas, 59
Currey, Brownlee O., Jr., 81
Davis, Louise, 57–58
Davis, Paul, 42, 52
Davis Cabinet Company, 103
Dickinson, Carrie, 92
Dick's Flowers, 130
Dobson, Allen, 57
Dobson, Mrs. Allen, 57
Dodge, Grenville M., 6
Donelson, Tenn., 130
Dortch, David D., 111
Dortch, Mrs. David D., 111
Dresden, Tenn., 119
Dudley, Guilford, Jr., 91
Dudley, Jane, 91, 114
Duncan Hotel, 9
Dunlap, Porter, **21**
Dunn, Betty (Mrs. Winfield), 75, 77–87, 92–93, 99; **77, 80, 83, 85, 127**
Dunn, Chuck, 77, 86; **77**
Dunn, Gayle, 77, 86; **77**
Dunn, Julie, 77, 83, 85–87; **77**
Dunn, Winfield, 75, 77, 79–87, 89–90, 93, 99, 128–29; **77–79, 83, 85, 126**
Dykeman, Wilma, 127
Earl, John, 69
East, E. E., 12
Echols, John Austin, 106
Eddy, Nelson, 43
Ehrhart, F. J., 53
Elam, Roy O., 47
Ellington, Ann. *See* Wagner, Ann Ellington
Ellington, Anna Catherine Cheek (Mrs. Buford), 65–69, 73–75, 83, 87, 105; **66, 74, 127**
Ellington, Buford, 62, 65–69, 73–75, 83, 87, 105; **63, 65–66, 73–74**
Ellington, John, 65
Elliston, Joseph T., 31

Ensworth School, 100
Esposito, Joe, 67
Evans, Silliman, 57
Evans, Mrs. Silliman, 57
Evins, Joe L., 68

Ewing, Andrew, 42, 47
Ewing, Elizabeth, 42
Faires, Ross N., 122
Faires, Mrs. Ross N., 122
Fall Creek Falls State Park, 87
Far Hills, 48, 52–53, 57; **xi, 50–52, 54–57**
Farris, William, 70
Farrell, Mrs. Norman, Jr., 31
Fayetteville, Tenn., 68
Finch, Ida, 101, 133
Flack, Debbie Blanton, 89, 95
Flack, Lewis D., III, 89
Fleming, Sam M., 82
Fleming, Mrs. Sam M., 82
Fogelman, Avron, 102, 105
Fogg, G. Malbourne, 12
Follin, Mary, 62
Follin, Webb, Jr., 62
Ford, Alma, 111, 131–32
Ford, Billy, 111, 130–32
Ford, Gerald, 106
Ford, Mrs. Gerald, 106
Ford, John, 128
Fort, Walter, 57
Fort, Mrs. Walter "Hank," 40, 56–57
Fortune, Beth, 130
Fowinkle, Eugene, 90
Fowinkle, Ruby, 90
Franklin, Tenn., 122
Franklin Road Academy, 95
Frazier, James B., 9
Frazier, Joe, 130
French, Charles, 89
Fuller-Cunningham Co., 53
Gaafar el Nimeiri of Sudan, 91
Gailor, Thomas F., 39
Gallatin, Tenn., 89
Gardner, W. H., 13
Geny Brothers Florists, 35
Glendale School, 70
Goodlow, Hallom W., **21**
Gordon, Anna, 16
Gore, Albert, Sr., 70; **60, 71**
Gore, Albert, Jr., 116; **111**
Gore, Tipper, 117
Gorrell, Frank, 72
Grace, Snake, 72
Graham, Billy, 61–62; **62**
Grand Junction, 131
Grand Ole Opry, 83, 112; **84**
Granger, Robert S., 6
Grant (playmate of Ben Jones Hooper), 19

Grant, U.S., 6
Gray, John M., Jr., 11–12
Gray, Mrs. John M., Jr., 12
Gray and Dudley Hardware, 11
Gulbenk, Mary Sue, 78–79
Gulbenk, Roupen M., 78–79, 93
Hailey, John, 111
Hailey, Mrs. John, 111
Hailsham, Lady, 113
Hailsham, Lord, 112–113
Haley, Alex, 106
Hankins, Mrs. Cornelius, 57
Hardin, Hal, 97
Harding, William Giles, 38
Harpeth Hall School, 86
Harris, Isham, 5; birthplace of, **6**
Hart, Donald, 57
Hart, Mrs. Donald, 57
Hart, Freeland & Roberts, 53
Hart, Russell, 53
Harwell, Coleman, 57
Harwell, Mrs. Coleman, 57
Harvard Law School, 42
Haslam, Jim, 122
Haslam, Natalie, 122
Hawkins, Alvin, 7, 18
Hayes, Hugh, 100
Hebrick and Lawrence, 53
Henderson, William I., 93
Henderson, Mrs. William I., 93
Henry Horton State Park, 38
H. E. Parmer Company, 53
Hermitage, The, 6–7, 16, 26, 40, 47, 73, 103; **127**
Hermitage Hotel, **39**
Historic Nashville, Inc., 57
Holman, Silena M., 16
Holt, Robert C. Jr., 56
Holyfield, Waylon, 129
Hooker, John Jay, 98–99, 129–130
Hooker, Tish, 98
Hooper, Anna B., 18–20
Hooper, Anna Bell Jones, 18–19
Hooper, Ben Jones, 19
Hooper, Ben W., 18–20; **18**
Hooper, Lemuel Washington, 19
Hooper, Newell Sanders, 19
Hooper, Randolph, 19–20
Horn-of-Plenty Garden Club, 93
Horton, Adeline Wilhoite, 36
Horton, Anna A. Wilhoite (Mrs. Henry), 36–38; **36**
Horton, Henry, 36–38, 75; **36**
Horton, John W., 36